healthy eating for
lower blood
pressure

Paul Gayler with
Gemma Heiser

healthy eating for
lower blood
pressure

For the first time, a chef and a nutritionist have teamed up
to inspire you with over 100 delicious recipes

Photography by Will Heap

Kyle Books

Dedication
To the many of you that suffer from high blood pressure but enjoy good food,
this book is for you.
Good health and good eating!!

Kyle Books
an imprint of Kyle Cathie Limited
Distributed by National Book Network
4501 Forbes Boulevard, Suite 200
Lanham, MD 20706
(800) 462-6420
general.enquiries@kyle-cathie.com
www.kylebooks.com

First published in Great Britain in 2010 by Kyle Cathie Limited

978-1-906868-28-4

A cataloging-in-publication record for this title is available from the Library of Congress

10 9 8 7 6 5 4 3 2 1

Project Editor: Judith Hannam
Design: geoffhayes@mac.com
Americanizer: Megan Schmidt
Copy Editor: Debra Stottor
Proofreader: Gill Lange
Indexer: Peter Lange
Photographer: Will Heap
Home Economists: Linda Tubby
Prop Stylist: Roisin Nield
Production: Gemma John
Color reproduction: SC (Sang Choy) International Pte Ltd
Printed and bound in Singapore by Star Standard Industries Pte Ltd

contents

foreword

Healthy Eating for Lower Blood Pressure is an excellent guide that can help reduce blood pressure and may also prevent hypertension. It correctly recomends cutting back on saturated fat, sugar, salt, calories, and eating poultry, fish, and lean cuts of meat, and lots of fruits and vegetables. These guidelines are quite similar to the DASH (Dietary Approaches to Stop Hypertension) eating plan, which has been especially effective in lowering blood pressure and in treating hypertension in the USA. It is also noteworthy that these dietary recommendations may reduce the amount of antihypertensive medication required to lower and/or maintain a normal blood pressure.

Paul Gayler, a renowned London Chef, and Gemma Heiser, a registered nutritionist and nutrition writer, who is experienced in health promotion, have joined forces to present a number of recipes that are not only delicious but also provide a healthy and balanced diet. These recipes are simple to reproduce, and, with modification, they can be used by patients with diabetes and by people trying to lose weight.

Healthy Eating for Lower Blood Pressure should be very helpful to people with pre-hypertension (blood pressures higher than 120/80) but not yet in the hypertensive range (140/90 or above), and those with primary hypertension (those with elevated blood pressure of unknown cause). By decreasing calorie intake and reducing consumption of calorie-dense foods and drinks, and by increasing calorie expenditure through additional physical activity, appropriate weight loss can be achieved. This is especially important in the US and UK, where obesity and its complications (hypertension, type 2 diabetes, abnormal blood concentrations of cholesterol and triglycerides, and many cancers) have generated a health crisis accompanied by an enormous financial burden on the public and governments.

Hopefully this book will reach the attention of those with hypertension and those who are overweight or who are suffering from complications of obesity—it provides valuable information for consuming a healthy diet that combats hypertension and/or obesity.

William M. Manger, MD, Ph.D.
Chairman, National Hypertension Association
Professor of Clinical Medicine,
New York University Medical Center
Emeritus Lecturer in Medicine,
College of Physicians and Surgeons

Dr. Manger is designated Distinguished Mayo Alumnus. He received the Mayo Clinic Alumni Association Humanitarian Award for combating childhood obesity.

a chef's prescription

Are you one of those people who think that healthy food can't possibly taste good? Does the idea of eating healthily instill fear and conjure up an array of images of dull, boring and uninspiring food, similar to rabbit food?

Sadly, healthy eating over the years has come to be associated with the vast amount of fad diets that don't do you any good at all. To me, there is no such thing as a diet, only a lifestyle change.

As a chef I love to cook, and I love to eat good food. I see no reason why a healthy diet should not be an interesting one. Eating is one of life's greatest pleasures and eating healthy foods should be as much fun as eating not-so-healthy foods.

However, we often find it difficult to make changes in our lives and our eating habits are no exception. We know in our minds that we should and could be eating better but often it seems like too much of a monumental upheaval and it's difficult to know where to start.

Eating healthily can benefit us all, but it is especially relevant for those with high blood pressure. What you eat can greatly affect your chances of developing high blood pressure and a healthy eating regime can both reduce the risk of developing it and lower a blood pressure that is already too high.

So what do we need to do to make healthy eating a reality?
It can be accomplished by simply changing our eating habits, varying the methods we use to cook and understanding how to get the maximum flavor from food. We need to be aware of the dangers of certain foods, especially those high in sodium, saturated fat and added sugar, and save them for a special occasion. There's no need to cut out all your favorite foods completely, like always denying yourself French fries in favor of yet another healthy green salad leaf! It is just about getting the balance right.

The main thing is to explore the incredible variety of healthy ingredients that are available to us and choose to eat them more often. Many types of fresh fish, together with fruit and vegetables are all nutritious foods just waiting to give endless variation to the food we eat everyday. Start by integrating small changes to your eating habits, ones that are easy to achieve and stick too, and before you know it you will be eating healthier and feeling better about yourself.

Cut back on those foods that give you saturated fat, added sugars and calories but little else. Choose leaner cuts of meat, such as low-fat chicken, fish and an abundance of fruit and vegetables and reduce salt in your diet by cooking with alternative spices and flavorings for really knock-out, delicious food.

This book sets out to inform and inspire you to experience new foods while at the same time improving your health. There is certainly no need to cook bland and boring dishes with the many options available in the book.

And one final note, all new things take time to adapt to, so be patient and change your diet gradually if you find that easier. Follow a balanced diet, make informed and healthy choices with everything that that you eat, at all times, whether it be a quick snack or a planned meal.

And most importantly, be careful not to over-analyze your diet as this will take all the pleasure out of good eating. Eat sensibly and you'll feel better for it.

Good health, bon appetit!!

Paul

introduction

High blood pressure is the biggest known cause of disability and premature death in the US through stroke, heart attack and heart disease. One in three adults in the US has high blood pressure and from 1996 to 2006 death rates from high blood pressure increased 19.5 percent. The condition also increases the risk of kidney and eye disease, dementia and other illnesses.

If your blood pressure is too high you may be very concerned about these risks. But the good news is there is a lot you can do to lower your blood pressure and keep it that way. Making some simple diet and lifestyle changes can have a real effect on your blood pressure and help you avoid these health problems in the future.

Even if you do not have high blood pressure, it is important to keep your blood pressure as low as you can. The lower your blood pressure the better for avoiding health problems in the future.

This book will show you how you can take control of your blood pressure and dramatically reduce your risk of a future stroke or heart attack.

about blood pressure

When your heart beats it pumps blood around your body to give it the energy and oxygen it needs. As the blood moves it pushes against the sides of your blood vessels. The strength of this pushing is your blood pressure.

If your blood pressure is too high it puts a strain on your body. Over many months and years this extra strain can cause damage to your heart and blood vessels which increases your risk of a stroke or heart attack.

When your blood pressure is measured it will be written as two numbers, for example 120/80mmHg. You would read this as "120 over 80" (mmHg stands for "millimeters of mercury" which are the units used to measure blood pressure). The two numbers show the highest and lowest pressures in your blood vessels:

● The first (or top) number is your systolic blood pressure. This is the highest level your blood pressure reaches when your heart beats.
● The second (or bottom) number is your diastolic blood pressure. This is the lowest level your blood pressure reaches between heart beats.

Both of these numbers are very important—the higher they are, the higher your risk of health problems in the future.

WHAT DO MY BLOOD PRESSURE NUMBERS MEAN?
Look at figure 1 to see what your blood pressure numbers mean. Find your top number (systolic pressure) on the left side of the chart and read across. Find your bottom number (diastolic pressure) on the bottom of the chart and read up. Where the two meet is your blood pressure.

Table 1 gives more detailed information on your blood pressure readings and what to do about them.

Figure 1
WHAT SHOULD MY BLOOD PRESSURE BE?
You can see from Table 1 health professionals agree that a healthy blood pressure is 120/80 or lower (but not below 90/60 which could mean you have low blood pressure). Lower blood pressure puts less strain on your heart and blood vessels, which reduces your risk of health problems.

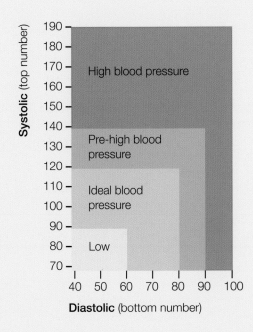

Systolic (top number)

190 —
180 —
170 — High blood pressure
160 —
150 —
140 —
130 — Pre-high blood pressure
120 —
110 — Ideal blood pressure
100 —
90 —
80 — Low
70 —

40 50 60 70 80 90 100

Diastolic (bottom number)

A person with a blood pressure of 115/75 has half the risk of having a stroke or heart attack as a person with a blood pressure of 135/85.

If your blood pressure is 140/90 or above you may have high blood pressure—consult with your doctor.

KNOW YOUR NUMBERS – GET CHECKED!

There are usually no symptoms of high blood pressure. Many people with high blood pressure do not know they have it – they have not thought to get their blood pressure checked because they feel perfectly well. This is why it is so important for you to know your blood pressure numbers. Having your blood pressure checked is simple, painless and allows you to take action before it is too late.

All adults should have their blood pressure checked at least every five years. If you have high blood pressure, or your readings are higher than they should be, you may need to have more frequent checks. Your doctor or nurse practitioner will advise you.

Table 1: What your blood pressure numbers mean

Your reading	What this means	What to do now
90/60 or below	You may have low blood pressure	Consult with your doctor
91/61 to 120/80	Your blood pressure is ideal	Follow diet and lifestyle advice in this book to help keep it at this ideal level
121/81 to 129/84	Your blood pressure is a little higher than it should be	Try to lower your blood pressure—follow the diet and lifestyle advice in this book
130/85 to 139/89	Your blood pressure is higher than it should be and could soon become high blood pressure	Try to lower your blood pressure as much as possible —follow the diet and lifestyle advice in this book
140/90 or above	You may have high blood pressure	Consult with your doctor. Follow the diet and lifestyle advice in this book

high blood pressure

Diagnosis

A single high reading of 140/90 or above does not mean you have high blood pressure. Many things affect your blood pressure so your doctor will take a number of readings at different times to see if it stays high. If your blood pressure is always 140/90 or more over time, your doctor will diagnose high blood pressure. Your doctor will also diagnose high blood pressure if only one of your readings is always higher than it should be. For example, if your blood pressure is 145/85 with only your top number (systolic pressure) being higher than it should be.

Causes

For a very small number of people with high blood pressure (around five percent) there is an underlying health problem which, if treated, can lower their blood pressure back to normal. Your doctor will rule out any underlying problems with a few simple tests.

But for most people there is probably no single cause of their high blood pressure. What we do know is that certain lifestyle factors put you at risk of developing the condition including:

- Eating too much salt
- Not eating enough fruit and vegetables
- Being overweight
- Not being active enough
- Drinking too much alcohol

There are some other factors you cannot control that also increase your risk of developing high blood pressure. These include having a family history of high blood pressure, your ethnicity, or getting older (the effects of an unhealthy lifestyle can build up over the years to put you at higher risk).

Treatment

For people with high blood pressure the aim is usually to get it down to 140/85 or below. But if you also have other health problems like kidney disease or diabetes, or you have had a stroke or heart attack, your doctor may advise you to aim for a lower target than this.

If you have high blood pressure, or your blood pressure is higher than ideal, making some diet and lifestyle changes could help you lower it back to healthy levels. However sometimes this is not enough. If this applies to you, you might also need to take medication to help lower your blood pressure further. You might also need to take medication if you have a higher risk of stroke and heart attack, for example if you smoke or have a family history of heart disease.

Even if you do need to take blood pressure medication you can still benefit from making changes to your diet and lifestyle, which could help your medication work better and reduce your risk of future health problems.

For more information on living with high blood pressure, including measuring blood pressure, treatment options and beneficial lifestyle changes see the The American Heart Association's website: www.heart.org

Key points
- High blood pressure increases the risk of stroke and heart attack if left untreated
- Lowering blood pressure as much as possible helps reduce your risk of future health problems
- This means making diet and lifestyle changes and taking medication if you need to

a healthy balanced diet

Eating a healthy balanced diet can benefit everyone but is especially important if you have high blood pressure. Making simple changes to your diet can lower your blood pressure and help reduce your risk of future health problems.

If your blood pressure is higher than it should be, making changes to what you eat could make all the difference between needing to take blood pressure medication and not. Or, if you already take them, it could help your medication work better so you might be able to reduce the dose or take less pills.

Eating a healthy balanced diet is not only important for your future health but can help make you feel much better in the short term too.

A BALANCED DIET
A healthy balanced diet includes:
● Plenty of fruit and vegetables—these should make up a third of your diet
● Plenty of starchy foods—these should make up another third of your diet
● Moderate amounts of lean meat, fish, eggs and other protein foods
● Moderate amounts of milk and dairy foods or dairy alternatives
● Limited amounts of food or beverages high in salt, saturated fat or sugar

Here are some tips to help you achieve the right balance:

1 Eat at least five portions of fruit and veg every day
Fruit and vegetables are an important source of vitamins, minerals and other nutrients and can help protect against many diseases. They can also help to lower your blood pressure. Choose a variety of different types and colors for greatest benefits. See the section "Eating More Fruit and Vegetables" for further advice.

2 Base your main meals on starchy foods
Starchy foods, also known as carbohydrates, include potatoes, bread, yams, squash, breakfast cereals, oats, pasta, rice and legumes such as lentils and chickpeas. They are a good source of energy, fiber, vitamins and minerals. Go for whole grain varieties when you can which usually have more nutrients and fiber.

5 Eat less salt

Eating less salt can benefit everyone and is really important if you have high blood pressure. Adults should consume no more than 2,300 mg of sodium a day and children even less. The next few pages focus on eating less salt.

6 Eat less fat and limit foods high in saturated fat

Too much fat in the diet can lead to weight gain (it contains twice as many calories as protein or carbohydrates), and too much saturated fat raises your blood cholesterol, which increases your risk of heart disease. Try eating some foods high in unsaturated fats instead, such as oily fish, avocados, unsalted nuts and seeds as these can help lower cholesterol. See the final section "Other Risk Factors" for more advice on fat.

7 Avoid added sugars in food and drinks

Cutting down on sugary foods and drinks may help you control your weight and is good for your teeth. In addition to obviously sweet products, watch out for added sugars in many convenience foods.

8 Drink plenty of water or other fluids

In the US, general guidelines recommend that you drink 1.9 liters (or eight 8-ounce glasses) of fluid every day. More if you do a lot of exercise.

9 Enjoy healthy food

Healthy food can be enjoyable and tasty—the recipes in this book are proof of that!

3 Eat at least two servings of fish every week

Fish is a good source of protein, vitamins and minerals. The omega 3 fats found in oily fish may help prevent heart disease. Try to eat at least one serving of oily fish each week such as salmon, trout or tuna (but no more than four servings a week, or no more than two servings if you are a woman who might have a child one day—see page 32).

4 Have some dairy (or dairy alternative) food every day

Milk and dairy are good sources of protein, vitamins and minerals and are the best source of calcium in the diet, which can help keep bones strong. In the US, there is no specific recommendation for how much dairy food to include in our diet but the Recommended Dietary Allowance (RDA) of calcium for healthy adults is 1,300 mg daily. Dairy, soy and dark green leafy vegetables are excellent sources.

DASH AND MEDITERRANEAN DIETS

You may have read about the "DASH" diet for lowering blood pressure and the "Mediterranean" diet for reducing risk of heart disease. There is some interesting evidence to support these diets. Both are broadly similar to the principles of a healthy balanced diet outlined in this book, including lots of fruits, vegetables and whole grain foods. The DASH diet also emphasizes cutting down on salt and eating low-fat dairy foods every day. The Mediterranean diet includes olive oil (an unsaturated fat) as the main source of fat in the diet and moderate amounts of wine.

You do not need to follow a specific dietary plan to lower your blood pressure unless your doctor has advised you to. The key diet and lifestyle changes you can make to help lower your blood pressure are:

- Eat less salt (no more than 2,300 mg a day)
- Eat more fruit and vegetables (at least five servings)
- Lose weight if you need to
- Be more active (aim for thirty minutes, five times a week)
- Drink alcohol in moderation (if at all)

DO I NEED SUPPLEMENTS?

Most people can get all the vitamins, minerals and other nutrients they need from a healthy balanced diet. There is currently no evidence to support the use of vitamin, mineral or herbal supplements to lower blood pressure. But if you do choose to take any, and you also take blood pressure medication, check first with your doctor because some supplements can cause unwanted effects when used in combination with medication.

eating less salt

Most people in the US eat too much salt. Adults should consume no more than 2,300 mg of sodium a day.

If you have high blood pressure, eating less salt is one of the best things you can do to help lower it. But even if you have normal blood pressure, cutting down on salt is a good strategy for helping you prevent high blood pressure as you get older. Eating less salt is important for the whole family.

SALT AND BLOOD PRESSURE
There is very good medical evidence that cutting down on salt will lower your blood pressure, whether you have high blood pressure or not.

How much salt should I eat?
The US government encourages limiting sodium consumption to 2,300 mg a day. This is a realistic rather than ideal target because most people consume an average of 3,400 mg or more. Health professionals recommend limiting sodium intake to 1,500 mg a day, which would have a greater effect on lowering blood pressure.

Studies have found that if people with high blood pressure consume just 1,500 mg less sodium a day they can lower their systolic pressure from between 3.6 to 5.6 mmHg and their diastolic pressure from between 1.9 to 3.2 mmHg. Eating 3,000 mg less sodium a day would double this effect. This might not sound like a lot but any drop in blood pressure is a drop in your long term risk of stroke and heart disease. Over time you could see even bigger falls if you combine eating less salt with other diet and lifestyle changes.

"Salt sensitivity"
Everyone can benefit from eating less salt but some people seem to be especially sensitive to the effects of salt on their blood pressure. Older people and those with a strong family history of high blood pressure seem to benefit even more than others from eating less salt. If this applies to you, consuming a lot less than 2,300 mg of sodium a day could make a really big difference to your blood pressure.

HOW TO CUT DOWN ON SALT
The problem with the US diet is not so much about the salt we add at the table or use in cooking, although you should try to cut down on this. The bigger issue is that **around seventy-five percent of the salt we eat is already in the food we buy.**

It can be difficult and time-consuming to work out exactly how much salt you eat—you would need to weigh all your food and calculate the amount of sodium in each item. Here are some easier, more practical ways to help you cut down:

1 Avoid or limit foods very high in sodium
Some foods or ingredients are obviously salty such as:

● Shrimp, anchovies, smoked or salted fish
● Smoked or processed meats like ham, bacon and canned meat
● Bouillon cubes and instant gravy mix
● Olives
● Soy sauce
● Snacks like chips, salted or dry roasted nuts
● Yeast extract

If you enjoy these foods it is not necessary to cut them out completely. Just try to save them for occasional treats on days when you will otherwise be mostly eating low salt foods. Or eat smaller amounts and look for low or reduced salt varieties.

2 Watch out for "hidden salt"
2,300 mg of sodium may sound like a lot but it can be surprising how much salt is "hidden" in food, it adds up quickly. One of the problems is that some foods containing salt do not taste obviously salty, for example:

● Bread, biscuits and bakery goods
● Some breakfast cereals
● Pre-packed lunch items like sandwiches, sushi and dressed salads
● Pesto, pasta and cooking sauces
● Pizzas and frozen meals

Table 2 "Hidden" salt in everyday food and beverages

	Portion size	mg of sodium per portion
Whole grain bread	1 medium slice	240 mg
Graham crackers	8 small pieces	190 mg
English muffin	1 muffin	200 mg
Cinnamon raisin bagels	1 bagel	390 mg
Carrot cake	1 slice (approx 1 oz)	125 mg
Bran flakes	1 average bowl (8 oz)	220 mg
crispy rice cereal	1 average bowl (8 oz)	240 mg
Tomato ketchup	1 tablespoon (15ml)	190 mg
Canned baked beans	Half cup (4 oz)	550 mg
Cheddar cheese	Small piece (1 oz)	190 mg
Packet of instant hot chocolate	1 packet as sold	170 mg

- Cheese (especially feta, parmesan, blue and processed cheeses)
- Table sauces, pickles and salad dressings
- Some soups (fresh, canned or powder mixes)
- Instant food or drinks like noodles and hot chocolate
- Some brands of baked beans
- Takeout food such as Chinese or Indian

Sodium-free or salt-free	less than 5 mg per serving
Low sodium	140 mg or less per serving
Reduced sodium	at least 25% less than reg version

Take a look at table 2 for examples of how much salt is "hidden" in some everyday products. Again, you do not need to cut out these foods altogether, especially bread, cereals and cheese, which provide important nutrients. Simply being aware that they add sodium to your diet can help you keep an eye on how much you are consuming each day.

Many manufacturers are gradually reducing sodium in foods sold in the US. Quantities given here were accurate at the time of going to press, taken from US product labels or website data.

3 Read the label
One easy way to cut down on salt is to check food labels and try to choose foods that are low in sodium. Read the Nutrition Facts labels on packaging to determine not only the amount of sodium in a product, but also it's Percent Daily Value. Aim for foods that are less than 5 percent of the Daily Value for sodium. Foods with a Percent Daily Value of 20 percent or more are considered high. Sodium is one part of salt (sodium chloride) and it is the sodium part that has an affect on blood pressure. Because sodium is also in other ingredients like monosodium glutamate and sodium bicarbonate, food labels have to give sodium rather than salt content.

Table 3 Salt savings: always check the label

Instead of...	Choose...	Sodium you could save...
Pepperoni pizza (1 slice)	Plain cheese pizza (1 slice)	300 mg
Frozen macaroni and cheese dinner (8 oz)	Spinach ravioli with tomato sauce (8 oz)	500 mg
1 grilled Italian sausage	1 grilled pork loin chop (4 ounces)	500 mg
Lobster roll	Poached salmon sandwich	520 mg
Smoked salmon (3.5 ounce)	1 grilled salmon steak (6 ounces)	800 mg
Club soda (8 ounce)	Seltzer water (8 ounces)	90 mg
1 breaded chicken breast fillet	1 plain skinless chicken breast	140 mg
Microwave popcorn (3.5 cups)	3 rice cakes	205 mg
1 instant breakfast shake	1 orange/banana smoothie	180 mg
French onion dip (2 tablespoons)	Greek yogurt dip (Tzatziki) (2 tablespoons)	150 mg
1 tablespoon tomato ketchup	1 tablespoon low-sodium ketchup	95 mg
Potato chips (1 ounce)	Dried fruit and unsalted nuts (1 ounce)	150 mg

4 Salt swaps
Comparing labels and swapping convenience foods for
more natural foods is a good way to eat less salt. Take a
look at table 3 to see how much sodium you could save by
making some straightforward food swaps.

5 Eat more natural foods and do not use salt in cooking
You can eat a lot less salt by replacing processed foods with
your own meals made with fresh and natural ingredients
(with no added salt)—try some of the recipes in this book.

Eating this way is not only better for you but it can be so much more tasty and satisfying too. When you cook there are many different ways you can flavor food instead of using salt or salty ingredients. For example, try using:

● Pepper, garlic, onions, chiles, lemon juice, fresh ginger, vinegar, herbs and spices

Be aware that some curry powders, spice and herb mixtures have added salt—check the label to be sure they are sodium free.

6 Get used to the taste of less salt
Enjoying food that tastes very salty is purely from habit. If you cut down on salt you could be surprised how quickly your taste buds adapt. You may even find after a few weeks you no longer like the taste of the salty foods you used to enjoy.

7 Children should eat less salt too
The amount of sodium children should consume is even less than adults. In the US, there are currently no established intake guidelines for children, simply to keep it as low as possible. In 2003, the United Kingdom did set target limitations. Table 4 illustrates their recommendations by age.

Babies below the age of one need only a tiny amount of sodium—their kidneys cannot cope with more than 400 mg per day.

Table 4 Maximum sodium intake for children

Age	No more than...
1 to 3 years	800 mg per day
4 to 6 years	1,200 mg per day
7 to 10 years	2,000 mg per day
11 and over	2,300 mg per day

Key points
● Eating less salt can help your lower blood pressure
● Consume no more than 2,300 mg of sodium a day —children should have even less
● Watch out for "hidden" sodium – seventy-five percent is already in the food we buy
● Read food labels—choose foods with less sodium
● Eat more natural foods—they usually have less sodium than processed foods
● Start to enjoy the taste of less salt—your taste buds will quickly adapt

There is good evidence that what children eat in early life influences their food choices when they are adults. If you encourage your children to eat less salt from an early age they are more likely to enjoy the taste of a lower salt diet when they are older. This will put them at lower risk of developing high blood pressure in the future.

Watch out for breakfast cereals, snack products and other processed foods aimed at children which are often high in sodium. Remember that children's favorites like tomato ketchup and sausages can also add a lot of sodium to their diet.

eating more fruit and vegetables

We should all be trying to eat at least five servings of a variety of fruit and vegetables every day. However most people in the US eat less than three servings a day.

There are many good reasons to eat lots of fruit and vegetables. There is good evidence for example that eating at least five servings a day can lower your risk of diabetes, obesity, stroke, heart disease and some types of cancer. Eating lots of fruit and vegetables can also help lower your blood pressure. They are a very good source of potassium, a mineral that has the reverse effect in the body to sodium. By eating at least five servings a day you will help your body get all the potassium it needs.

As well as protecting your future health you can gain instant benefits from eating more fruit and vegetables. They are mostly low in fat and calories so they can help you control your weight. And because of all the important vitamins, minerals, fiber and other nutrients they contain, eating more fruit and vegetables can boost your energy and help you feel better every day.

16 grapes
2 or more smaller fruits e.g. plums, tangerines
8 strawberries
A handful of dried fruit e.g. raisins
1 medium fruit e.g. apple, orange, banana, pear
½ large fruit e.g. avocado, grapefruit*
1 large slice of a large fruit e.g. melon, papaya, pineapple
1 glass (8 ounces) of 100% fruit or vegetable juice or smoothie
2 large celery stalks
1 cereal bowl of mixed salad leaves
1 medium fresh tomato or 7 cherry tomatoes
Half a bell pepper

Table 5 Example portion sizes

* Grapefruit juice can effect the action of some medicines – ask your doctor if you should avoid it, especially if you take statins or calcium channel blockers. Other fruit juices are fine.

HOW MUCH DO I NEED?

The United States Department of Agriculture (USDA) gives specific guidelines depending on age and gender, but overall approximately 3 cups of vegetables and 2 cups of fruit are recommended daily. Table 5 gives examples of what counts as a cup.

THE FOOD PYRAMID

The Food Pyramid was first adopted by the USDA in 1992 to replace earlier food group classification systems. In April 2005, the USDA released "Dietary Guidelines for Americans" and an updated Pyramid design, both of which encourage physical activity and the omittance of the previously existant "Fats, Oils and Sweets" food group.

For more information on the Food Pyramid and on how to get your Recommended Daily Allowance of fruit and vegetables visit www.mypyramid.gov

Can supplements provide the same benefits?

Studies that have looked at taking nutrient supplements (vitamins and minerals for example) have mostly concluded they do not have the same beneficial effects as eating fruit and vegetables. It appears that fruit and vegetables have a unique mix of vitamins, minerals, fiber and other nutrients that work together to protect our health in a way that supplements cannot replicate.

WHAT COUNTS

All fresh, frozen, chilled, canned and dried fruit and vegetables count. Fruit and vegetables found in dishes like soup, stews and convenience foods also count but it is best to avoid those with a lot of added salt, saturated fat or sugar.

Variety is important

Different fruit and vegetables provide a different mix of vitamins, minerals, antioxidants and other nutrients. Therefore it is important to try to eat a variety of different types each day.

Juice, smoothies and pulses

100% fruit or vegetable juice and smoothies can count towards your daily allowance. But fruit juice can only count as one of your portions per day no matter how much you drink. This is because fruit juice contains less of the beneficial nutrients found in whole fruit such as fiber, and the high levels of natural sugars in juice can be bad for your teeth. The same applies to legumes such as lentils and chickpeas. These can count towards your daily allowance but again only as one portion a day. Remember that legumes also count as starchy foods which are an important part of a healthy balanced diet.

Potatoes do not count!

Potatoes and other starchy root vegetables like yucca, yams and plantains do not count towards your daily allowance They are of course vegetables, but because they are an important source of carbohydrates, they count as starchy foods instead.

CHILDREN SHOULD EAT MORE TOO

The Recommended Daily Allowance for children is the same, or slightly less, than adults depending on the child's age. Children should be encouraged to eat a variety of produce every day. Doing so will help develop their taste buds and make them more likely to eat fruit and vegetables as adults.

TIPS ON GETTING ENOUGH

5 cups may sound a lot to achieve but it's surprising how easy it can be to make it a healthy new habit. If you have one or two portions at each main meal and snack on fresh fruit you can easily reach your five or more cups a day.

Here are a few ideas to help you eat more fruit and vegetables:

● Add fruit to your cereal or oatmeal—try sliced banana, apple or fresh or frozen berries
● Blend any fruit you like with a touch of juice or low-fat yogurt for a healthy smoothie
● Snack on raw vegetable sticks with reduced-fat hummus
● Add lettuce and tomato to your lunchtime sandwich

- Add vegetables, lentils or beans to stews or casseroles
- Make fresh soups or stir fries using lots of vegetables

GETTING THE MOST FROM YOUR FRUIT AND VEG

To get the most from fruit and vegetables try to:
- Choose mostly natural fruit and vegetables—convenience foods such as vegetable curries, canned fruit or ready-to-roast vegetables often have lots of added salt, fat or sugar
- Buy fresh fruit and vegetables in season and grown locally—they are likely to contain more vitamins
- Eat lots of different colored fruit and vegetables each day to get the best range of nutrients
- Choose canned or frozen fruit and vegetables without added sugar or salt

Preparing and cooking vegetables
The way you prepare and cook vegetables can affect the amount of vitamins left in them and their salt, fat and calorie content. Here are some tips to help preserve vitamins and keep your vegetables healthy:

- Steam vegetables when possible
- Chop vegetables immediately before cooking—do not leave them sitting in water
- Eat vegetables as soon as they have been cooked
- If you boil vegetables cut them into larger chunks and cook in as little water and for as short a time as possible
- If you fry or roast vegetables do not add oil or use just a tiny amount of an unsaturated oil (such as olive oil)—vegetables absorb fat during cooking
- Avoid adding salt to vegetables when cooking or serving them—try pepper or herbs instead

Key points
- Eating more fruit and vegetables can help lower your blood pressure
- Fruit and vegetables help protect against a range of diseases
- Eat at least five cups a day—aim to eat a variety of different types and colors

healthy weight

Around two out of three adults in the US are above their ideal weight. Being overweight puts a strain on your heart and can increase your blood pressure. Losing weight if you need to is a very effective way to lower your blood pressure and has other important health benefits too.

Losing weight is not always easy. A huge industry has built up around dieting which tries to tempt us with quick fix solutions to losing weight. But while some "fad" diets may seem to work in the short term, most people quickly put the weight back on when they go back to their usual eating habits.

The key to losing weight and keeping it off is to make small, gradual changes to what you eat that you can keep up for life, and to be more active if you can.

DO I NEED TO LOSE WEIGHT?
If you are not sure if you could benefit from losing weight you can use waist and body mass index (BMI) measurements as useful guides.

Waist measurement
Your waist measurement is a measure of how much fat you carry around your middle—if you carry excess fat here you are more likely to suffer health problems from being overweight.

You can measure your waist with a tape measure. Place it round your midriff roughly at the level of your belly button. You are at more risk of developing health problems if your waist measures:

● Women: 35 inches or above
● Men: 40 inches or above

Body Mass Index (BMI)
The BMI is a guide to whether you are the right weight for your height. To work it out you can use one of the many BMI calculators found on the internet (try www.cdc.gov). Or use the following equation: BMI = weight (lbs) / [height (in)]^2 x 703.

The following is a guide to what your BMI means:
BMI less than 18.5: underweight
BMI between 18.5 and 24.9: healthy weight
BMI between 25 and 29.9: overweight
BMI of 30 or above: obese

If your BMI is 25 or more you are at increased risk of health problems. And the more overweight you are the greater the risks. If your BMI is 35 or above you may need specialist help to manage your weight and health—visit your doctor or nurse practitioner for advice.

However, this BMI applies only to adults and is not the best measurement for everyone. For example it is not suitable for those with well-developed muscles such as athletes.

Calculating the BMI for children and teens follows the same formula, however the interpretation of the results is quite different. This is because the amount of body fat in children varies by age and also differs between girls and boys. A Child/Teen BMI calculator is available online at www.cdc.gov

BENEFITS OF LOSING WEIGHT
There are many good reasons to lose weight if you need to. For example, it can help:

● Lower your blood pressure
● Reduce your risk of stroke, heart disease and some types of cancer
● Manage your diabetes (or reduce your risk of developing it)
● Improve back and joint pain
● Improve your sleep
● Improve your mood
● Improve your fertility
● Boost your energy so you can enjoy life to the fullest
Consider why you want to lose weight. For example, would

you like to have more energy or less joint pain so you can play with your grandchildren? It is a good idea to write down your reasons for wanting to lose weight. They can act as a reminder when you are finding it tough to keep going.

HOW TO LOSE WEIGHT
If you are overweight you have taken in more calories (energy) from food and drinks over the years than your body has used up. To lose weight you need to reverse this.

Successful and long term weight loss means making sensible and healthy changes to your diet (so you eat less calories) and being more active (so you use up more calories). See the next section for advice on being more active.

Here are some tips to get you started:

1 Set yourself a realistic goal
It is important to set yourself a goal that is achievable so you are less likely to be disappointed and give up. Health experts believe that losing five to ten percent of your body weight is a realistic target to aim for. This can bring about positive health benefits such as lower blood pressure.

2 Take it slowly
Those who lose weight slowly, say one to two pounds each week, tend to be more successful at losing weight and keeping it off. If you lose weight more quickly you might be losing muscle rather than fat, which is not a healthy way to lose weight.

Each pound of body fat contains roughly 3,500 calories. To lose a pound a week you need to eat 500 calories less a day or be more active and use up 500 calories more a day (or ideally a combination of the two).

Making small and gradual changes to what you eat and being more active can really add up to make a big difference to your weight over time.

3 Try not to think of it as "going on a diet"
Try not to get too obsessed with food or think of it as "going on a diet". Focus instead on achieving a healthy balance in your diet. This way you can take in fewer calories overall by eating lots of fruit and vegetables and whole grain starchy foods and cutting down on high fat and sugar foods which contain a lot of calories.

It can take a lot of time and effort to lose weight. What you eat every single day is not so important as how much you eat in total over the weeks and months ahead.

4 Do not restrict food groups

Some popular diets encourage you to cut out whole food groups like carbohydrates (starchy foods). Any diet that restricts fruit, vegetables or whole grain starchy foods is not a healthy way to lose weight—you will not get the full range of nutrients you need.

The reason most people lose weight on these "fad" diets is that they simply eat less than they usually would. You can get the same effect in a much more healthy way by eating a balanced diet with less fat and sugar and by being more active.

5 Get some support

Some people feel they need an eating plan to help them lose weight or the support of others. It is a good idea to visit your doctor or nurse practitioner—they can let you know of support available in your area, for example if there is a dietitian who could help you or a local support group.

Commercial weight-loss programs are helpful for some people. But remember the goal is to make small, lifelong changes—make sure the program offers help with sustaining a healthy weight long term, not just with how to lose it initially.

If you do not enjoy being in a group there are many websites with information and tools to help you staymotivated including:

www.mypyramid.gov
www.americanheart.com
www.cdc.gov
www.webmd.com
www.helpguide.org

SMALL CHANGES ADD UP

Small changes you make to your diet and activity levels can really add up over the months ahead to help you lose weight and keep it off. Here are some tips on changes you could make to help you lose weight the healthy way:

Control your appetite

● Do not skip breakfast—research shows it helps people maintain a healthy weight
● Eat at regular times during the day to avoid overeating if you get too hungry
● Go for brown or whole grain foods with lots of fiber which are more filling
● Have some protein with main meals such as lean meat, fish, eggs, lentils or beans
● Be careful if you drink alcohol—it can make you feel more hungry and adds calories too
● Drink plenty of water—being dehydrated can be mistaken for hunger

Eat less fat

● Choose reduced-fat dairy foods such as 1% milk and lower fat spreads
● Remove visible fat or skin from meat before cooking
● Grill, poach, steam, bake or broil instead of frying or roasting in oil

Other ways to cut calories

● Plan meals and snacks ahead of time so you always have healthy food at hand
● Compare food labels of similar products—go for those with less calories
● Reduce your portion sizes—try using smaller plates and bowls if it helps
● Pile up your plate with vegetables—they are filling and low in calories
● Replace high-calorie snacks with fresh fruit
● Drink less sugary drinks

Key points
● Losing weight if you need to is an effective way to lower your blood pressure
● Losing weight has many other positive benefits for your health and wellbeing
● The best way to lose weight is to make lifelong changes to what you eat and be more active

being active

The majority of adults in the US do not do enough physical activity. Being inactive can have a major, negative impact on your health.

Adults who are physically active have around a thirty percent reduced risk of premature death and up to a fifty percent reduced risk of developing heart disease, stroke, diabetes, some types of cancer and other illnesses.

In the short term being more active can help to lower your blood pressure and improve your cholesterol levels. It can also help you sleep better, have more energy, feel less stressed and reduce your risk of depression and anxiety. And being more active is one of the best ways to lose weight and keep it off when combined with a healthy balanced diet.

What is an active lifestyle?
The US government recommends doing thirty minutes of at least 'moderate intensity' activity on five or more days of the week. Moderate intensity means any activity that gets you warm and makes you breathe a bit faster. For children and teens the recommendation is sixty minutes a day.

Whatever your age, young or old, being more active in your day-to-day life can make you feel better and lowers your risk of health problems in the future.

ACTIVITY AND BLOOD PRESSURE
Exercise causes a temporary rise in blood pressure and when you stop exercising your blood pressure should return to its usual resting levels. But in the long term being more active can help to reduce your blood pressure levels overall.

It is a good idea to check how safe it is for you to take up any new activity, especially if you are new to exercise or have just been diagnosed with high blood pressure. Your doctor or nurse practitioner can advise. If you have very high blood pressure (200/110 or above) always check first.

If you have high blood pressure you should avoid any type of exercise that causes a quick rise in your blood pressure or places strain on your heart. This includes weight lifting, sprinting and playing squash. Scuba diving and parachuting can also be dangerous – always check with your doctor first.

WHAT IS THE BEST TYPE OF EXERCISE?
Unless you enjoy it you do not need to do strenuous gym workouts or take up running. It is better to try to fit some activity into your daily routine that you enjoy and will keep up in the long term. For example, you could walk or bicycle to work instead of driving. Or take up an active hobby like bowling, dancing, or gardening.

You can do your thirty minutes of activity in stretches of ten minutes or more. For example three ten minute walks in a day could have as much benefit as one thirty minute walk. Build up gradually until activity becomes a normal part of your daily routine.

Exercise that is good for your heart
High blood pressure is a risk factor for heart disease. So if you have high blood pressure it makes sense for you to do the types of exercise that can improve the condition of your heart and blood vessels. This means doing some aerobic exercise that gets you a little out of breath such as brisk walking, jogging, dancing or swimming.

Exercise that is good for your bones
It is a good idea to also do some weight-bearing exercise to help protect your bones. In young adults this helps maintain the density and strength of bones. In older adults it helps to slow the loss of bone that tends to happen with age—this helps prevent osteoporosis, a condition which increases the risk of broken bones.

Weight-bearing exercise includes brisk walking, skipping, dancing, aerobics, playing tennis or jogging, or any other activity where you support the weight of your own body.

Activities for older people

It is important to remain active when you are older. Activities that help build your strength, coordination and balance can help you maintain your mobility, independence and ability to do everyday tasks. It can also help reduce your risk of falling and getting injured.

To avoid injury you should avoid higher intensity activities or any activity that involves sudden or complicated movements, unless you are used to these types of exercise.

Exercise and mobility

If you are unable to get up unaided from a chair you could ask your doctor about chair-based exercise classes in your area. These can help you gently build up your fitness.

HOW TO BE MORE ACTIVE

Here are some ideas to help you get more active for life:

● Take up an active hobby like golf or bowling
● Find a "gym buddy"—having a friend to exercise with can make it more fun
● Schedule a walk into your daily routine, for example walk around the block at lunchtime
● Make it a family affair—play a game of basketball with the kids or enjoy a bike ride after dinner
● Join a walking group—the American Volkssport Assocation has clubs across the country. www.ava.org
● Get your hands dirty—gardening is a good way to keep active
● Yoga, T'ai Chi and pilates can keep you supple and help your posture and balance—many community centers and fitness clubs offer classes
● Remember that everyday activities such as housework and climbing stairs count too

Key points

● Being active helps lower blood pressure and reduces your risk of other health problems
● Aim to be active for at least thirty minutes on five days of the week
● Aim for moderate intensity activity which gets you a bit warm and a little out of breath
● To keep your heart healthy try to fit in some aerobic exercise
● Being active is important for all ages, young or old

alcohol

Drinking too much alcohol increases your risk of high blood pressure and other health problems too. In the US nearly one in three adults drink too much alcohol. In other words they regularly drink more than the recommended daily limit of:

● Two drinks a day for men
● One drink a day for women

A drink is defined as 12 ounces of beer, 4 to 5 ounces of wine and 1.5 ounces of spirits. Limits for women are lower because of their smaller body size and different body composition, with more fat and less water to dilute alcohol. It is advisable for pregnant women, or those trying to get pregnant, to avoid alcohol altogether.

Benefits of moderate alcohol consumption

For many of us drinking alcohol is a normal part of our lives and there can be some benefits to drinking it. It can help you relax and unwind for example. And drinking moderate amounts (one or two a day) seems to protect against heart disease in men over the age of forty and post-menopausal women. But that is not to say you should drink alcohol to protect your heart—eating a healthy diet, being active and giving up smoking can bring about much greater benefits.

Risks of regular over-drinking

People who drink too much alcohol tend to have raised blood pressure. Regularly drinking more than is recommended also increases the risk of other health problems like stroke, heart and liver disease, and probably raises the risk of mental health problems like depression and anxiety. Alcohol also increases the risk of some types of cancer including mouth and breast cancer.

If you do choose to drink alcohol it is important to stay within recommended limits to help keep your blood pressure levels healthy and reduce your risk of future ill health.

BENEFITS OF CUTTING DOWN

Most people who suffer health problems from alcohol are not alcoholics. Rather they are people who regularly drink more than is recommended over a number of years. This causes a build-up of damage in the body over time, resulting in health problems in the long term.

You can gain many short and long term benefits from cutting down on alcohol if you regularly drink more than is recommended. For example, it could:

● Lower your blood pressure and risk of stroke
● Reduce your risk of some types of cancer and other diseases
● Help you feel better and improve your mental wellbeing
● Improve your sleep
● Give you better skin
● Boost your fertility
● Help you lose weight if you need to
● Improve your sex life – alcohol can cause temporary impotence in men

UNITS OF ALCOHOL

It is important to be aware that the strengths of many alcoholic drinks, for example wine and beer, have increased in recent years, as have serving sizes. Because of this it is easy to underestimate how much you drink. Table 6 gives examples of some alcoholic drinks and the actual number of servings they contain.

Type of drink	No of Servings
1.5 ounces Gin (40%) and tonic	1 serving
Standard glass (6 ounces) red, white or rose wine (13%)	1.3 servings
1 pint of beer (4%)	1.3 servings
Half bottle (13 ounces) of wine (13%)	3 servings
Flute of Champagne (6.5 ounces) (13%)	1.4 servings

BINGE DRINKING

You have probably seen a lot of media coverage on the "binge drinking" culture in the US. Binge drinking means reaching a state of intoxication during any one drinking session.

Binge drinking is roughly defined as the consumption of 5 or more servings for men and 4 or more servings for women, generally consumed within a two hour period. If you look at Table 6 and the number of servings in many drinks, you can see how easy it can be to exceed these amounts— a woman drinking three standard glasses of wine (6 ounces) would actually be drinking about 4 servings of alcohol.

Binge drinking is particularly bad for health as it can greatly increase blood pressure in the short term and risk of stroke. It is much better to stay within the maximum daily limits of alcohol servings than to "save them up" for one or two heavy drinking sessions. This is why the government recommends a daily maximum number of servings rather than a weekly maximum.

TIPS FOR CUTTING DOWN

If you think you should try to drink less, here are some practical ways to do this:

- Aim to have a few alcohol free days each week
- Try low alcohol options like low strength beer
- Alternate alcoholic drinks with water or low-cal soft drinks
- Dilute drinks like white wine with water or soda
- Sip your drink slowly and drink lots of water to keep hydrated
- Avoid salty snacks when drinking—they make you thirsty so you are likely to drink more
- If you drink too much alcohol wait 48 hours before having any more to help your body recover

If you think that you, a friend or family member might have a problem with alcohol, you could visit your doctor for advice. There are also many organizations offering help and advice in the US including:

Alcoholics Anonymous: www.aa.org

The National Institute on Alcohol Abuse and Alcoholism: www.niaa.nih.gov

Key points
- Drinking alcohol is a personal choice and moderate drinking can have positive health benefits
- Women should drink no more than 1 serving a day; men no more than 2 servings a day
- Drinking too much alcohol can increase your blood pressure and risk of other health problems
- Binge drinking is especially bad for your blood pressure and health

other risk factors

Coronary heart disease (CHD) is the name given to the gradual narrowing of blood vessels in the body that can lead to angina and heart attacks. It is the single most common cause of death in the US. High blood pressure is one of the major risk factors for CHD. Other known risk factors include:

Factors you cannot change
- Getting older
- Gender (men are at greater risk at an earlier age)
- Family history
- Ethnicity (Risk is higher for African-Americans, American Indians and Mexican-Americans)

Factors you can change or manage
- High blood pressure
- High cholesterol
- Smoking
- Diabetes
- Obesity
- Physical inactivity
- Drinking too much alcohol

If you have more than one risk factor your risk of CHD is much increased. So if you have high blood pressure it makes sense for you to keep your cholesterol levels healthy and to stop smoking too, as well as making the diet and lifestyle changes already outlined in this book.

CHOLESTEROL

High levels of cholesterol in your blood increases your risk of developing CHD and stroke. Diet and lifestyle factors play a major role in your risk of developing high cholesterol as well as its treatment.

Cholesterol and heart disease

There are several types of cholesterol in the body. Scientists believe that the two main types related to risk of heart disease are High Density Lipoprotein (HDL) and Low Density Lipoprotein (LDL).

If you have high levels of LDL (also known as "bad cholesterol") this can lead to narrowing and blockage of your blood vessels which could eventually lead to a heart attack, stroke or other complications.

Higher levels of HDL cholesterol (also known as "good cholesterol") seem to be protective against heart disease. The reasons are not yet clear but low levels of HDL seem to be an important risk factor for heart disease in North American and European adults. Being physically active can help increase your HDL cholesterol levels.

There is another type of fat in the blood called triglyceride. If you have high triglyceride levels and low HDL cholesterol you are at higher risk of CHD. Obesity is a major cause of this. Losing weight and being more active can help reverse this risk factor.

Healthy cholesterol
The only way to know if your cholesterol levels are healthy is to have a blood test. If you have high blood pressure or any other risk factors for heart disease it is a good idea to ask your doctor, nurse or pharmacist for a cholesterol check.

If your cholesterol levels are on the high side of normal or they are too high, it is likely your doctor will ask you to make some changes to your diet and lifestyle. Your doctor might also prescribe cholesterol-lowering medicines.

CHANGING YOUR DIET TO LOWER CHOLESTEROL
Eating a balanced diet with lots of fruit and vegetables and whole grain starchy foods can help keep your cholesterol levels healthy. Other lifestyle factors like being physically active, not smoking, keeping to a healthy weight and not drinking too much alcohol are also very important.

Other specific aspects of your diet you can change to help lower your cholesterol levels include:

1 Eat less saturated fat
Some cholesterol is already in foods we eat such as liver or eggs. But the much greater problem is the cholesterol made in our bodies from the saturated fat in our diet. Cutting down on saturated fat is very important for lowering your cholesterol and keeping it at healthy levels.

Animal fats, coconut and palm oil are all sources of saturated fat. Foods that tend to be high in saturated fat include:
- Fatty cuts of meat
- Processed meats
- Butter, ghee, shortening
- Full fat dairy foods
- Pastries, cakes, cookies
- Snacks and chocolate

Eating less of these foods will help you cut down on saturated fat. Try to also avoid eating visible fat or skin on meat, and swap full fat dairy foods for reduced fat versions.

Food labels
You can also cut down on saturated fat by comparing food labels and trying to choose products with a low amount of saturated fat (or eat much smaller amounts of foods with a high amount). Look at the amount of "sat fat" in grams, as well as the percent of Daily Value. As a general rule:

Low saturated fat	5% Daily Value (DV) or less
Medium saturated fat	between 5% and 20% DV
High saturated fat	more than 20% DV

2 Include some unsaturated fat in your diet
Unsaturated fats (including polyunsaturated and monounsaturated oils) can help reduce cholesterol levels and lower your risk of heart disease.

Foods that contain unsaturated fats include:
- Oily fish (see next page)
- Avocados
- Nuts and seeds
- Sunflower oil
- Olive oil
- Spreads made with mono- or polyunsaturated oils

3 Eat more oily fish

Oily fish is the best source of omega 3 fat, a type of unsat-urated fat that can lower triglyceride levels and help prevent heart disease. Oily fish include salmon, trout, mackerel, sardines and herring. Try to eat at least one portion a week.

Sustainability of fish populations is an important environ-mental issue—try to choose sustainably sourced fish when you can. To find out more see the NOAA Fisheries Service Website at: www.fishwatch.noaa.gov

There are limits on how much oily fish we should eat due to environmental pollutants that build up in them. Boys, men and women who will not have a child in the future can eat up to four portions a week. Girls or women who are pregnant, breastfeeding or might have a child one day should have no more than two portions a week. You can find more information on recommended limits in the US and further advice on oily fish and pregnant women on the USDA's website: www.mypyramid.gov

Research indicates that omega 3 fats found in vegetable sources like flaxseed (linseed) oil do not have the same beneficial effects as those from oily fish. They can still be included as part of a healthy diet and may be a useful alternative for vegetarians not wishing to take fish oils.

4 Eat foods high in soluble fiber

Soluble fiber in the diet can help lower cholesterol levels. Soluble fiber is found in:
- Oats
- Legumes like lentils and beans
- Some fruits and vegetables

5 Use products fortified with plant sterols or stanols

You could try having foods with added plant sterols or stanols. The American Heart Association recommends that the use of foods containing sterols be reserved for adults requiring lower total and LDL cholesterol levels because they are at high risk of, or have had, a heart attack.

smoking and heart disease

Smoking is the leading preventable cause of premature death in the US. Smokers are at much greater risk of having a heart attack than non-smokers. Stopping smoking is the single best thing you can do to avoid a future heart attack and prevent other diseases like lung cancer.

It is never too late to give up smoking. Visit your doctor or nurse to find out about services available locally to help you quit. There are many organizations in the US that can offer advice and support on stopping smoking including:

National Cancer Institute: www.smokefree.gov
(Toll free hotline: 1 877 44U QUIT)
The American Heart Association (www.heart.org)
The American Cancer Society: www.cancer.org
(Toll free hotline: 1 800 ACS 2345)

To summarize the changes you can make to lower your blood pressure and reduce your risk of a future heart attack, stroke or other health problems:

1 **Eat less salt: no more than 2,300 mg of sodium a day (much less is better)**
2 **Eat more fruit and vegetables: at least five cups of a variety every day**
3 **Lose weight if you need to: make small changes to your diet that you can keep up for life**
4 **Be more active: aim for thirty minutes at least five times a week**
5 **Drink alcohol sensibly: no more than 1 serving a day for women; 2 servings a day for men**
6 **Eat oily fish: at least one portion a week**
7 **Lower your cholesterol: eat less saturated fat, more unsaturated fat and some soluble fiber**
8 **If you smoke: seek help to quit**

Remember, small steps can lead to big changes in the months and years ahead that can lower your blood pressure and dramatically reduce your risk of health problems in the future.

essential equipment

A kitchen with the following equipment will not only encourage a healthier style of cooking but also, in turn, make the job easier and your results more successful.

Always buy the best-quality equipment you can afford. It will do the job better and should last a lot longer too.

● Good-quality, heavy-based pots and pans of varying sizes. In general, I suggest using non-stick pans as they allow you to reduce the amount of fat you use in cooking without causing food to stick. You also need deep-sided pans for braising, which are then also suitable for oven use.

● A grill pan or flat griddle for grilling. There are some special low-fat grills on the market now that drain away the cooking fat. In the summer, take advantage of your barbeque as it will cook vegetables and meat in particular with incredible flavor.

● Heavy-bottomed casserole dishes or similar ovenproof dishes with lids for braising and stewing.

● Good-quality deep-sided non-stick woks for low-fat stir-frying, which enable you to use very little fat when cooking.

● Non-stick roasting pans of varying sizes.

● Non-stick baking pans and flat baking sheets.

● Small steamer unit (or small Chinese steamer baskets).

● A centrifugal juicer is one of my favorite pieces of equipment; great for extracting the maximum juice from fruit and vegetables as well as retaining healthy vitamins.

healthy cooking methods for healthy eating

When you are trying to establish healthy eating habits, how you cook your food is just as important as what food you eat.

The cooking methods described below are the best for retaining flavor, nutrients and good all-round health.

GRILLING
Grilling is a fast and extremely healthy way to cook, as it uses minimal fat in the process.

Using a preheated grill pan or outdoor grill gives a delicious smoky flavor to foods. Alternatively, use a grill rack placed under a conventional broiler.

By marinating in advance, or using an oil-water spray, foods can be grilled using little or no fat.

ROASTING / DRY ROASTING
Roasting is a cooking method that uses dry heat in an oven. Buy the leanest possible meat available for roasting and cook food on a wire rack inside a roasting pan so that any fat drains away during cooking.

I advise using non-stick roasting pans, thereby using minimal fat at all times.

Meats, fish and vegetables are delicious roasted and roasting helps retain valuable vitamins and nutrients in the food.

Dry roasting is usually reserved for such foods as nuts, spices and seeds.

Herbs may also be added to foods as they roast, adding flavor to the food.

BAKING

This is another excellent healthy cooking method, great for cooking smaller pieces of fish and vegetables, as well as fruits. Again I suggest using non-stick baking pans for the job.

STEAMING

One of the healthiest and simplest ways to cook low-fat dishes, as foods require no fat. The food is placed in a perforated basket and suspended above simmering water. You can add different seasonings to the water to add flavor if you wish. Steaming is particularly good for cooking vegetables as it retains more nutrients than any other cooking technique.

Nowadays you can buy Chinese steamers with multi-level baskets which are ideal for cooking more than one food at once.

BOILING / POACHING

When boiling foods, especially vegetables, use only a minimum of water in the saucepan, (except when cooking pasta), this way the nutrients in the food do not leach out into the water and lose valuable nutrients such as vitamins.

Poaching involves gently simmering foods in water or flavorful liquids until cooked and is a great way to cook fish, and poultry. You will need a deep-sided pan, deep enough to submerge the ingredients. The liquid should not boil.

BRAISING

Braising entails cooking food, meat, poultry, fish or vegetables slowly in a small amount of liquid at low heat in a tightly covered pot, usually in the oven.

Before braising, food is often quickly pan-seared to obtain color before being cooked in wine, stock or sauce. It is a great way to cook the tougher cuts of meat.

PAN-FRYING / STIR-FRYING

Pan-frying is a fast and efficient way to cook and seal in flavor but it is not the healthiest method as foods are fried in fat. However, using a non-stick pan will keep the amount of fat used down to a minimum as it requires little or no fat for the task.

When frying, I generally use olive, canola or sunflower oil as they are high in unsaturated oils and low in saturated fat while also adding flavor. A non-stick cooking spray or oil-water spray is also suitable for the job.

Stir-frying became popular some years ago with our interest in asian foods and cooking. It is quick, uses very little or no fat at all and preserves the freshness and color of food, especially keeping vegetables crunchy and retaining the juices in meat and fish.

Stir-frying is a great way to get your recommended daily allowance of vegetables.

Use a deep-sided non-stick wok or deep-sided non-stick frying pan.

MICROWAVE

Microwave cooking is a good low fat method, particularly good for vegetables as it requires only a small amount of liquid for cooking, thus retaining all the nutrients as well as color and texture.

PG tips

Here are a few do's and don'ts which you will find useful for eating more healthily and for controlling your blood pressure by using little or no salt.

do's

● Avoid adding salt to your cooking and to your food at the table by enhancing the natural flavors of your dishes with herbs, spices such as onion, garlic (which may play a role in lowering blood pressure), lemon juice, flavored vinegars, chiles, tomatoes and fruits. Use fresh herbs whenever possible, dried herbs are fine but often have a "grassy" taste when used in dishes. Some herb blends contain added salt so always check the list of ingredients on the label.

● Use marinades as a way of adding flavor to your cooking. Marinating meat, fish and vegetables in ingredients such as low fat yogurt, spices, herbs, citrus juices and flavored vinegars will all add moisture and flavor.

● In dishes requiring the use of cream, use low-fat milk instead and thicken it in sauces with a little cornstarch. In general use low or reduced-fat dairy products, such as milk, yogurts and cheeses.

● Cook vegetables without adding salt and in a minimum of boiling water so that they retain their natural flavor and nutrients. Alternatively steam them which is a healthier option, as is roasting, baking and stir frying. Whichever method you employ, always serve them immediately once they are cooked.

● When using canned vegetables, beans or fruit, always rinse them under cold running water to remove the excess salt used in their production or, better still, buy products with no added salt which are often available in supermarkets.

● Use more vegetables and fruits that are rich in potassium such as asparagus, beets and bananas. Potassium-rich food and beverages are important elements in decreasing blood pressure, as it has the opposite effect in the body to sodium (the part of salt which can increase blood pressure).

● Satisfy your sweet tooth with the natural sweetness of fruit. Ideally eat fresh fruit, although canned and dried fruits are also good and still count towards your Daily Allowance.

● Do check labels on certain foods that you may at first think don't contain salt, such as breads or cereals, as many do contain a lot of sodium. Always choose whole grain bread as opposed to white bread as it has more fiber.

● Always trim all visible fat from meat and skin from poultry.

● Many of your favorite recipes call for butter or oil. Using unsaturated oils such as olive, canola or sunflower oil or a reduced fat spread instead lowers the amount of saturated fat in a particular dish. I do not generally use a lot of reduced-fat spreads in my recipes as I find it can noticeably change the taste of the food. The use of non stick cooking pans reduces the need for using lots of oil in cooking.

● Another successful medium for low fat cooking is the use of a oil-water based spray for pan frying, grilling or roasting. Simply mix together $2/3$ olive or canola oil and $1/3$ water in a spray bottle. The oil mix can also be enhanced by infusing the oil with herbs or spices for added flavor. There are also cooking sprays available commercially, if preferred.

● In general look for ingredients and foods that contain little salt, but which provide your diet with plenty of vitamins, minerals and other nutrients.

● In the real world, it is not always possible to cook from scratch and there may be a need to buy prepared foods. Take the time to check food labels on foods which give healthier choices and are low in salt, sugar and saturated fat and high in fiber. For example, commercially made bouillon cubes can be rather salty in taste, so rather than using them, purchase a low-sodium packaged stock, available in boxed form from leading supermarkets or, as a last resort, use half a bouillon cube to the same quantity of water.

don'ts

● Steer away from processed foods when possible, including fruits, fish, meat and vegetables that come ready-prepared in sauces. These often contain a lot of added salt, sugar and fat.

● By paying attention to the labels on food, you can reduce your sodium intake dramatically.

● Once fresh vegetables have been prepared, never leave them uncovered and exposed to the air, or leave them soaking in water as their natural vitamins dissolve in the water and are lost.

● Try not to add sugar to fruits or salt to vegetables when you cook or serve them.

● There are numerous lower-sodium salt-alternatives on the market nowadays (though they often contain MSG to enhance the flavor). I personally find their taste unacceptable and advise you not to use them. In the long term, your healthiest option by far is to give up using salt completely in your cooking. You may find it difficult at first. I suggest you reduce your intake gradually as soon your taste will adapt and you will find you don't miss it. The answer is to persevere!

the healthy kitchen pantry

By using this list as a guideline you can create most of the recipes in this book and many more besides.

IN THE FRIDGE
Low-fat natural yogurt
Low-fat milk
Reduced-fat crème fraîche
Low- or reduced-fat cheese
Low- or reduced-fat salad dressing
Reduced-fat mayonnaise
Reduced-fat spreads
Eggs
Fruit juices, freshly squeezed
Lean cuts of meat, fish and shellfish
Various freshly prepared low-sodium stocks

FRUIT AND VEGETABLES
A wide variety of fruit and vegetables is essential for good health. Most fruit and vegetables are a good natural source of potassium and low in sodium, for example:

Asparagus
Beets
Carrots
Celery
Zucchini
Mushrooms
Peas

Green beans
Potatoes
Tomatoes
Sweet corn, corn on the cob
Onions
Garlic
Squashes, various types
Fennel
Spinach
Leeks

Banana
Apples
Pears
Lemons
Limes
Oranges
Pineapple
Blueberries
Nectarines
Peaches
Mango
Pomegranate
Melon
Watermelon
Figs
Soft red and black fruits
Rhubarb
Prunes

HERBS AND SPICES

Fresh herbs and spices are essential in low-fat cooking as they add color and flavor. They are excellent in marinades and for replacing salt in recipes overall.

FRESH HERBS

Basil
Tarragon
Chives
Cilantro
Mint
Thyme
Oregano
Sage
Flat-leaf parsley
Dill

Coriander (ground, seeds)
Cumin (ground, seeds)
Cardamom (ground, pods)
Cinnamon (ground, sticks)
Nutmeg
Chile (fresh, flakes, powder)
Curry powder (try to find a brand with no added salt)
Black pepper (ground, whole)
Mustard (fresh, powder, seeds)
Saffron
Paprika (sweet, smoked)
Turmeric
Ginger root (fresh, ground)
Fennel seeds
Fresh lemongrass
Vanilla (pods, extract, essence)

CANNED AND PACKAGED PRODUCTS

When choosing canned and packaged products, look for brands with no added salt or sugar.

Oil-water spray
Cooking spray

Various flavored low-sodium bouillon cubes
Reduced-fat coconut milk
Tomato paste
Chopped canned tomatoes
Canned sweet corn
Canned fruits, various types
Couscous, various cereals
Dried beans
Dried fruits, various types
Fruit juices (cranberry, tomato, apple, peach nectar)
Olives in brine
Capers in brine
Whole grain pastas
Rices
Flavored vinegars (sherry, balsamic)
Olive, canola, sunflower oil
Sesame oil
Vanilla pods
Various jams, reduced-sugar
Reduced-salt soy sauce
Tahini
Honey, maple syrup
Whole grain flour
Cornstarch
Mango chutney

NUTS, SEEDS AND GRAINS

Hazelnuts
Almonds (slivered, ground)
Cashews
Pistachio nuts
Pumpkin seeds
Sesame seeds
Sunflower seeds

Wheatgerm
Coconut flakes
Rolled oats

chapter one
breakfast & brunch

baked bean rarebit

For you baked bean lovers out there, and I know there are many, here is a great breakfast combo: baked beans on toast with a twist, topped with a cheesy rarebit crust on thick whole grain toast—absolutely delicious.

14 ounces dried navy beans, soaked overnight, then drained
1 onion, finely chopped
1 tablespoon dark brown sugar
1 tablespoon black molasses
1 x 14-ounce can diced tomatoes
2 tablespoons tomato paste
1 garlic clove
1 tablespoon white wine vinegar

For the rarebit
2½ tablespoons 1% milk
2 ounces cheddar cheese, grated
1 teaspoon English mustard
1 large egg, beaten
pinch of paprika
4 thick slices whole grain bread, toasted

Serves 4

Place the beans in a large pan, cover with 4 times their volume of cold water and boil for 10 minutes. Reduce the heat, partly cover the pan and simmer for 1–1½ hours or until the beans are tender (this can be done well in advance if preferred).

Preheat the oven to 325°F. For the bean mixture, place the beans in an ovenproof casserole dish, add the remaining ingredients and mix together thoroughly. Cover with a lid, place in the oven and bake for 1 hour or until the beans form a thick sauce around them (add a little water while cooking if necessary).

For the rarebit, heat the milk, cheese and mustard together in a small pan over a low heat, until the cheese has melted. Add the beaten egg and stir until the mixture thickens, about 2 minutes. Do not overcook the egg or it will scramble. Season with the paprika.

Top each slice of toast with a pile of the beans and finally with some of the rarebit and place under the broiler until golden. Sprinkle with black pepper and serve.

4 PORTIONS: 504 CALORIES, 33G PROTEIN, 9G FAT, 3.7G SATURATED FAT, 78G CARBOHYDRATE, 15.5G SUGAR, 20.4G FIBER, 337MG SODIUM

broiled pink grapefruit with cinnamon

A simple but tasty breakfast recipe. The better the quality of your honey, the better it will taste. Look for a creamy variety as runny honey tends to melt before it has time to caramelize. Pink grapefruits have more flavor and aroma than their yellow-skinned counterparts.

2 tablespoons creamed honey (alfalfa or clover preferably)
1 teaspoon ground cinnamon
2 large pink grapefruits

Serves 4

Heat the honey and cinnamon over low heat for 5–8 minutes, then remove from the heat and leave to infuse for up to 2 hours.

Cut the grapefruit in half horizontally. Separate the segments from the membranes, using a grapefruit knife (or small knife), to cut around the outside. To help your grapefruit stand firmly, cut a thin slice of peel horizontally from the base of each half.

Preheat the broiler. Spread the cinnamon and honey mixture equally over the 4 grapefruit halves. When the broiler is really hot, broil the grapefruit for 4–5 minutes—they should become lightly caramelized. Allow to cool slightly before serving.

4 PORTIONS: 54 CALS, 0.9G PROTEIN, 0.1G FAT, 0G SATURATED FAT, 13.2G CARBOHYDRATE, 12.5G SUGAR, 1.3G FIBER, 4MG SODIUM

baked potato and porcini omelette

Porcini mushrooms are a gourmet-style mushroom, a real autumn treasure, not easily found unless you know where to find them and pick your own. Dried can be more readily available, but if not you can use thick slices of button mushrooms instead.

3½ ounces fresh porcini mushrooms (or ⅔ ounce dried)
3 tablespoons olive oil
1¼ cups new potatoes, washed but not peeled, thinly sliced
1 small garlic clove, crushed
½ red chile, seeded and finely chopped
2 tablespoons chopped fresh flat-leaf parsley
4 free-range eggs
4 egg whites
freshly ground black pepper

Serves 4

Preheat the oven to 350°F.

If using dried porcini, place them in a small bowl, cover with warm water and leave to soak for 45 minutes. Remove, drain well and dry them in a cloth. If using fresh, thinly slice.

Heat half the olive oil in a medium non-stick pan, add the potatoes and cook until golden and cooked through. Remove from the pan and set aside.

Add the mushrooms and remaining oil to the pan and saute until golden, then add the garlic and chile and cook for another 2 minutes. Return the potatoes to the pan, toss together with the mushrooms and parsley.

Take 4 individual ramekins or other shallow ovenproof dishes and lightly brush with a little olive oil. Spread the potato and mushroom mixture over the base of each dish.

Place the eggs and egg whites in a bowl, add a little black pepper and whisk until well combined. Divide the egg equally between the 4 dishes and bake for 40–45 minutes. Leave to cool for a minute before serving.

4 PORTIONS: 244 CALS, 13G PROTEIN, 15G FAT, 3G SATURATED FAT, 14G CARBOHYDRATE, 1.2G SUGAR, 1.9G FIBER, 168MG SODIUM

granola

This wholesome breakfast cereal is popular with people of all ages. You could add a handful of raisins to the finished granola if you like, or try my summer-inspired version. Lovely served with fresh fruit and a good dollop of yogurt. This granola can be stored in an airtight container for up to a month.

½ cup rolled oats
¼ cup wheatgerm
¼ cup sunflower seeds
¼ cup sesame seeds
⅓ cup slivered almonds
2 tablespoons sunflower oil
4 tablespoons honey
2 tablespoons brown sugar
1½ teaspoons vanilla extract
⅓ cup desiccated coconut

Serves 8

Preheat the oven to 350°F.

In a bowl, combine the oats, almonds, wheatgerm, sunflower seeds, sesame seeds and sliced almonds.

In a pan, heat the oil with ⅓ cup warm water, add the honey, brown sugar and vanilla extract and almost bring to the boil. Pour over the ingredients in the bowl.

Stir the mixture well, then spread onto a large baking sheet in a thin, single layer. Place the tray in the oven and bake for 15 minutes, tossing the mixture regularly to achieve even coloring. Add the coconut, mix well and bake for another 15 minutes. Remove from the pan and leave to cool.

4 PORTIONS: 646 CALS, 17G PROTEIN, 43G FAT, 10G SATURATED FAT, 51G CARBOHYDRATE, 24.2G SUGAR, 9.2G FIBER, 18MG SODIUM

summer granola

When the summer comes around my granola takes on a different character, dusted with lavender sugar on top of wonderful ripe berries.

To make lavender sugar, take 3 tablespoons superfine sugar and mix with 1 teaspoon dried lavender flowers, place in a sealed jar and leave to infuse, ideally for up to 2 weeks, although it is fine to use immediately.

poppy seed pancakes with ginger fruits and mint syrup

Typically we think of pancakes as stacks piled tall and drizzled with maple syrup. Stop! Let's make way for thin French-style crêpes, which make an unusual breakfast. See my tips for making them in advance. This also makes a great late-morning brunch. For the best results, leave the pancake batter to rest for 30 minutes before cooking; this allows the starch cells to expand, producing lighter pancakes.

For the batter
3½ ounces whole grain flour
1 cup 1% milk
1 egg yolk
1 egg
1 tablespoon sunflower oil,
  plus a little for frying
1 tablespoon poppy seeds

For the filling
2 tablespoons honey
juice of ½ lemon
1 cinnamon stick
1¼ cups mixed, ready-to-eat dried fruits
  (e.g. apricots, figs, dates and golden raisins)
2 tablespoons preserved ginger in syrup,
  finely chopped
3 tablespoons pine nuts, toasted
2 tablespoons chopped fresh mint
confectioners' sugar for dusting

Serves 4 (makes 12 pancakes)

For the batter, place the flour in a bowl, make a well in the center, add the egg and egg yolk, the oil and a little of the milk. Whisk the flour into the liquid then gradually blend in the rest of the milk until the batter is smooth and free from lumps. Stir in the poppy seeds and leave covered for 30 minutes.

Cut the fruit into small ½-inch cubes, place in a pan with the honey, lemon and cinnamon and cook over medium heat for 10–12 minutes. Lift out the fruit and set aside, turn up the heat and boil the liquid for another 5 minutes until syrupy in consistency.

Heat a little sunflower oil in an 8-inch heavy-based crêpe pan or non-stick pan. Pour in enough batter (from a pitcher or use a ladle) to thinly cover the base of the pan, swirl the batter around the pan to thinly cover the base of the pan. Cook for 1 minute until small holes appear in the pancake. Use a spatula to flip (or for those a little more daring, toss it over) and cook for another minute. Slide onto a cutting board.

Repeat this method until all the batter has been used (it should make about 12 pancakes). As you make the pancakes stack them on a plate, cover with foil and keep them warm in a low oven. If you prefer to make your pancakes in advance, place the cooked pancakes on an plate, cover them in plastic wrap, and refrigerate until ready to use.

To serve, spoon a little of the fruit mixture onto a quarter section of each pancake, fold in half then in half again, to create little pockets. Place on serving plates, drizzle over any excess mint-infused syrup, dust the plate with confectioners' sugar and serve immediately.

4 PORTIONS: 514 CALS, 11.9G PROTEIN, 21.3G FAT, 3.8G SATURATED FAT, 73.5G CARBOHYDRATE, 54.2G SUGAR, 4.5G FIBER, 167MG SODIUM

congee with scallions and ginger

I have recently become interested in the origins of the Asian breakfast. At the Lanesborough we offer dim sum, scallion pancakes, steamed buns and rice porridge, known as congee. I prefer it simple and plain but often we serve it topped with chicken or fish. Congee is classically served with "Yutao," a sort of fried bread doughnut that is available from Asian stores, but I always serve it with some chopped ginger and chopped red chile, which is very popular in China.

7 ounces jasmine or short grain rice
1 garlic clove, crushed
¾-inch piece ginger, peeled and finely chopped
2 tablespoons reduced-salt soy sauce
2 scallions, thinly sliced

Serves 4–6

Bring 8½ cups of water to the boil in a heavy-based saucepan. Add the rice, the garlic and half the ginger and bring to a boil.

Reduce the heat and simmer gently for 1 hour until the rice is well overcooked and almost puréed—it should be like oatmeal in consistency.

Add the remaining ginger and the soy sauce and stir throughly. Pour into 4 soup bowls, sprinkle the scallions on top and serve.

4 PORTIONS: 172 CALS, 4G PROTEIN, 0G FAT, 0G SATURATED FAT, 41G CARBOHYDRATE, 0.9G SUGAR, 0.3G FIBER, 356MG SODIUM

jewelled oatmeal

As I have gotten older I find more often that I choose oatmeal as my preferred breakfast dish, especially on cold mornings. It is not only warming and filling, it is also simple to prepare. This recipe has a touch of the exotic about it, tempting and altogether beautiful to the eye. To remove the seeds from the pomegranate, place halves into a bowl of water, the seeds will sink and the white pulp membranes will float.

2 ounces dried apricots (or canned), cut into small dice
2 tablespoons raisins
1 ounce dates, finely diced
2 tablespoons pistachio nuts (or sliced almonds)
1 fresh pomegranate, halved, seeds removed,
   drained and dried in a cloth (see above)
1 cup rolled oats
4 cups 1% milk
1 teaspoon orange flower water (optional)
3 tablespoons maple syrup or honey

Serves 6

In a bowl, soak the dried apricots (if using) and raisins in warm water for 1 hour until they swell in size. Drain.

Place the raisins, dates, apricots and pistachios and pomegranate in a bowl and toss together.

Place the oats and milk in a saucepan and bring to a boil, stirring constantly. Lower the heat, simmer for 3–4 minutes until thickened, and add the orange flower water if desired.

Divide the oatmeal into 4 individual serving bowls and top each with a pile of the fruit mixture. Drizzle over a little maple syrup and serve. ·

6 PORTIONS: 296 CALS, 11G PROTEIN, 8G FAT, 2.5G SATURATED FAT, 48G CARBOHYDRATE, 25.7G SUGAR, 4G FIBER, 84MG SODIUM

a few of my favorite wake-up shakes and juices

Sometimes I wake up and all I need is a refreshing breakfast juice or smoothie. At the hotel we prepare numerous, here are a few that get me motivated in the morning.

strawberry yogurt and passion fruit shake

4 small passion fruits, halved
½ cup fresh strawberries, cut into small pieces
⅔ cup low-fat strawberry yogurt
1 tablespoon wheatgerm
1 cup chilled 1% milk
honey, to taste

Serves 4

Scoop out the seeds and flesh of the passion fruit and place in a blender along with the strawberries. Add the yogurt, wheatgerm and milk and blend until smooth and creamy in texture. Add the honey to taste, pour into chilled glasses and serve immediately.

4 PORTIONS: 109 CALS, 6G PROTEIN, 2G FAT, 1G SATURATED FAT, 17G CARBOHYDRATE, 15.4G SUGAR, 1.4G FIBER, 72MG SODIUM

pineapple, coconut and banana lassi

1 medium pineapple
1 banana
½ cup coconut milk
¾ cup 1% milk
juice of 1 lemon
pinch of ground cinnamon
honey, to taste

Serves 4

Remove the outer skin of both the pineapple and banana and cut into small pieces. Place in a blender with the coconut milk, lemon juice and cinnamon and blend until smooth and creamy in texture. Add the honey to taste—this will vary depending on the sweetness of your pineapple.

Chill for 30 minutes in the fridge for best results, pour into glasses and serve.

4 PORTIONS: 190 CALS, 3.6G PROTEIN, 5.5G FAT, 4G SATURATED FAT, 33.9G CARBOHYDRATE, 33G SUGAR, 2.8G FIBER, 73MG SODIUM

raspberry and orange smoothie

1½ cups fresh raspberries
4 oranges, halved
sugar, to taste

Serves 4

Place the raspberries in a blender along with the freshly squeezed juice of the oranges and blend until smooth and creamy. Add sugar to taste, again depending on the sweetness of your fruits. Transfer into chilled glasses and serve.

4 PORTIONS: 90 CALS, 3G PROTEIN, 0G FAT, 0G SATURATED FAT, 20G CARBOHYDRATE, 20.4G SUGAR, 4.3G FIBER, 10MG SODIUM

watermelon and pomegranate juice

1¼ cups juicy ripe watermelon
¾ cup pomegranate juice, with no added sugar if possible
juice and zest of 2 limes
crushed ice

Serves 4

Remove the outer skin of the watermelon and cut the flesh into small pieces. Place in a blender with the pomegranate juice, lime juice and zest and blend until smooth. Transfer to chilled serving glasses, add some crushed ice and serve.

4 PORTIONS: 52 CALS, 0.6G PROTEIN, 0.2G FAT, 0G SATURATED FAT, 12.8G CARBOHYDRATE, 12.8G SUGAR, 0.1G FIBER, 2MG SODIUM

carrot, apple and ginger energizer

4 large carrots, peeled and cut into small chunks
4 Granny Smith apples, cored and cut into small chunks
1-inch piece ginger, peeled, finely grated

Serves 4

Pass all ingredients through a juicer. Chill in the fridge for up to 30 minutes before serving to allow the flavors to infuse. Stir well as it tends to separate, then divide between 4 chilled glasses, and serve.

4 PORTIONS: 143 CALS, 2G PROTEIN, 1G FAT, 0G SATURATED FAT, 35G CARBOHYDRATE, 33.8G SUGAR, 6.6G FIBER, 39MG SODIUM

prune and orange compote with orange pekoe

Orange Pekoe is the term used to describe a range of black teas, normally associated with China and Sri Lanka. Orange Pekoe does not indicate the tea's flavor, rather the size of the tea leaf, with Orange Pekoe being the largest, fullest grade. Here it forms a lovely syrup for a traditional prune compote.

1 cup prune juice (no added sugar)
2 orange pekoe tea bags (or loose-leaf tea)
10 ounces ready-to-eat prunes
2 juicy oranges
2 tablespoons chopped hazelnuts
low-fat plain yogurt (optional)

Serves 4

Bring the prune juice to the boil in a small saucepan. Remove from the heat, add the pekoe tea and leave to infuse, uncovered, for 10 minutes.

Strain through a fine strainer into a bowl, add the prunes, cover with plastic wrap and leave to steep overnight in the fridge.

Cut away the outer skin and white pith from the oranges, then cut into slices over a bowl to catch the juices (be sure to remove any pits).

To serve, remove the prunes from the fridge, place in individual bowls and top with the orange slices. Add the reserved orange juice to the prune syrup and pour over the prunes and oranges. Scatter with hazelnuts and serve with a little yogurt if desired.

4 PORTIONS: 203 CALS, 3.7G PROTEIN, 3.6G FAT, 0.2G SATURATED FAT, 41.4G CARBOHYDRATE, 41.3G SUGAR, 5.6G FIBER, 21MG SODIUM

banana-stuffed french toast

As a child I never remember having eaten French toast, as it was not the sort of thing we liked to eat. I often prepare it now as a weekend treat, usually covered with an array of colorful, soft berries or stuffed with crushed ripe bananas.

4 slices thick-cut whole grain bread, halved diagonally
1 large banana, ripe
2 eggs, beaten
½ teaspoon ground cinnamon
½ cup 1% milk
1 tablespoon low-fat crème fraîche
1 tablespoon soft brown sugar
1 tablespoon grated orange zest
2 tablespoons confectioners' sugar, plus extra for dusting
2 teaspoons sunflower oil
4 tablespoons warm maple syrup, to serve (optional)

Serves 4

Using a sharp knife, make an incision into the side of each cut slice of bread, being careful not to cut right through. Peel the banana and mash it in a bowl. Using a spoon, carefully fill each incision with the mashed banana and lightly press down to secure the filling.

Whisk the eggs, cinnamon, milk, crème fraîche, brown sugar, orange zest and confectioners' sugar in a bowl.

Heat the oil in a non-stick pan over a moderate heat. Gently dredge each slice of banana-stuffed bread in the egg mix and cook for 2–3 minutes on each side until golden.

Transfer to serving plates, drizzle with maple syrup, if desired, and serve.

4 PORTIONS: 255 CALS, 9G PROTEIN, 8G FAT, 2G SATURATED FAT, 40G CARBOHYDRATE, 21.7G SUGAR, 2.5G FIBER, 159MG SODIUM

portobello mushroom kedgeree

Kedgeree is believed to have been brought back to England during Victorian times by British colonials returning from India. An ancestor of the widely diverse "hash" family, our version features the wonderfully succulent and meaty portobello mushroom.

2 tablespoons olive oil
8 large portobello mushrooms, thickly sliced
1 small onion, finely chopped
1 teaspoon mild curry powder
¼ teaspoon ground turmeric
4 cardamom pods, shelled, seeds removed
1¼ cups basmati (or brown basmati) rice,
   rinsed under cold running water for
   5 minutes, then drained
2½ cups hot vegetable stock (see page 156;
   if using packaged stock or bouillon cubes use
   "low salt" varieties)
2 tablespoons roughly chopped cilantro
2 hard-boiled eggs, peeled and quartered (optional)

Serves 4

Heat the oil in a heavy-bottomed, deep-sided, non-stick pan. When hot add the mushrooms and cook for 4–5 minutes until golden.

Add the onion, curry powder, turmeric and cardamom seeds and cook for a further 2–3 minutes to allow the spices to become fragrant.

Add the rice to the pan and mix well. Pour in the hot stock, stirring well, bring to a boil, cover with a lid and simmer over low heat for 15–18 minutes or until the rice is tender and all the liquid has been absorbed.

Transfer to a large serving dish, sprinkle with cilantro and garnish with the hard-boiled eggs if desired.

4 PORTIONS: 300 CALS, 9G PROTEIN, 7G FAT, 1G SATURATED FAT,
53G CARBOHYDRATE, 1.3G SUGAR, 3.5G FIBER, 31MG SODIUM

herb roasted vine tomatoes and mushrooms on toast

I often top these tomatoes and mushrooms with a poached egg, which when cut oozes out over the herby tomatoes.

4 large portobello mushrooms, cleaned
2 tablespoons olive oil
1 teaspoon chopped fresh rosemary
1 teaspoon lemon thyme (or regular thyme)
½ teaspoon grated lemon zest
1 tablespoon balsamic vinegar
14 ounces cherry tomatoes on the vine
4 whole grain English muffins

Serves 4

Preheat the oven to 400°F.

Place the mushrooms on one side of a non-stick baking pan, drizzle with half the olive oil, then sprinkle with the herbs, lemon zest and balsamic vinegar. Roast for 10 minutes. Add the cherry tomatoes on the other side of the pan and roast for another 5 minutes until all are softened.

Toast the muffins under a broiler until golden on both sides. Top each muffin with a roasted mushroom and a cluster of the roasted cherry tomatoes.

Drizzle any remaining pan juices over the tomatoes and serve.

4 PORTIONS: 243 CALS, 10G PROTEIN, 8G FAT, 1.1G SATURATED FAT, 35G CARBOHYDRATE, 4.5G SUGAR, 2.1G FIBER, 444MG SODIUM

rhubarb and plum breakfast parfait

Seasonal fruits make for a wonderful breakfast treat at any time. This is my take on a simple yogurt parfait that's delicious and easy to make. Experiment with your favorite fruit combinations.

½ cup wheatgerm
½ cup unsweetened apple juice
1¼ cups rhubarb, chopped into 1-inch pieces
1 cup plums, pits removed and cut into large chunks
1 tablespoon confectioners' sugar
¼ cup low-fat plain yogurt, plus extra to serve
2 tablespoons slivered almonds, toasted
small mint leaves, for garnish

Serves 4

Place the wheatgerm and apple juice in a bowl, cover with plastic wrap and refrigerate overnight.

Place the rhubarb and plums in a pan with the sugar and ¼ cup of water, cover and bring to the boil. Reduce the heat to a simmer and cook for 4–5 minutes. Remove from the heat and set aside to cool.

Add the honey and yogurt to the soaked wheatgerm.

Divide half the wheatgerm mixture between 4 attractive parfait glasses, then top with half the rhubarb and plum compote. Repeat with the remaining wheatgerm mixture and compote. Top with a spoonful of yogurt, sprinkle with the sliced almonds and garnish with mint, if desired.

4 PORTIONS: 188 CALS, 9.8G PROTEIN, 5.5G FAT, 0.3G SATURATED FAT, 26.5G CARBOHYDRATE, 19.1G SUGAR, 6.3G FIBER, 21MG SODIUM

chapter two

soups & salads

avocado soup with three-onion salsa

A creamy, rich and velvety avocado soup, just the dish to serve on a warm summer night. Look out for the dark green, rough-skinned Hass variety of avocado; it has a less waxy feel than the bright green Fuerte.

2 large ripe Hass avocados
1 cup cold vegetable stock (see page 156; if using packaged products or boullion cubes use "low-salt" varieties)
1 cup cold 1% milk
4 scallions, chopped
juice of 2 limes
pinch of ground cumin
freshly ground black pepper
Tabasco sauce

For the salsa
2 scallions, finely chopped
1 tablespoon chopped chives
1 small shallot, finely chopped
juice of 1 lime
1 tablespoon maple syrup

Serves 4

Cut the avocados in half lengthways and remove the pits. Peel then place in a blender with the stock, milk, scallions and lime juice. Process until smooth.

Season with ground cumin, black pepper and Tabasco, pour into a bowl, cover with plastic wrap and refrigerate for 30 minutes before serving.

For the salsa, mix all the ingredients together in a bowl and season with a little black pepper.

Divide the soup into 4 chilled soup bowls and top each with a mound of salsa in the center.

4 PORTIONS: 262 CALS, 5G PROTEIN, 23G FAT, 3.3G SATURATED FAT, 9G CARBOHYDRATE, 7G SUGAR, 4G FIBER, 45MG SODIUM

potato, wild garlic and sorrel soup

Wild garlic, or ramsons, (*Allium ursinum*) grow in woodlands with moist soil, and is easily identified by its garlic-like smell and long leaves. It grows from late winter but is at its best in spring. The flavor is similar to garlic, but slightly milder. It's also great in salads, especially towards the end of the season when they burst into bloom with tiny white flowers.

2 tablespoons canola oil
2 small leeks, chopped
1 onion, chopped
1 cup wild garlic leaves, chopped
2 medium potatoes, peeled and cut into small pieces
1 quart vegetable stock (see page 156; if using packaged stock or boullion cubes use "low salt" varieties)
½ cup 1% milk
¼ cup sorrel leaves, torn into small pieces
freshly ground black pepper

Serves 4

Heat the oil in a heavy-bottomed saucepan, add the leeks, onion and chopped wild garlic and cook for 6–8 minutes until the vegetables soften.

Add the potatoes and stock and bring to the boil. Reduce the heat and simmer for 25–30 minutes until the potatoes are cooked.

Transfer to a blender and process until the soup is smooth. Return the soup to the heat and add the milk and sorrel. Stir until wilted, season with black pepper and serve.

4 PORTIONS: 147 CALS, 6G PROTEIN, 7G FAT, 0.8G SATURATED FAT, 16G CARBOHYDRATE, 5.2G SUGAR, 3G FIBER, 52MG SODIUM

billy bi soup (spiced mussel soup)

This classic French soup made from mussels, saffron and curried spices is utterly delicious and quite addictive. The majority of the mussels available in the US are farmed rather than wild these days. Ensure that your mussels are plump in size and that the shells are tightly closed when buying them. I recommend you eat mussels on the day of purchase.

2½ cups fish stock (see page 156; if using packaged products or bouillon cubes use "low-salt" varieties)
good pinch of saffron
1 tablespoon olive oil
1 small leek, finely chopped
1 garlic clove, crushed
1 teaspoon mild curry powder
4 tablespoons dry white wine
2 ounces fresh mussels, cleaned
½ cup 1% milk
2 teaspoons cornstarch (mixed with 2 teaspoons cold water)
2 tablespoons chopped fresh chervil (or flat-leaf parsley)
freshly ground black pepper

Serves 4

In a pan, bring the stock and the saffron to a boil, then leave to infuse over very low heat for 8–10 minutes.

Heat the oil in a large saucepan, add the leek and garlic and cook for 2 minutes. Add the curry powder, cook for 1 minute, then add the white wine and boil rapidly for 2 minutes.

Throw in the mussels and add the hot saffron stock. Return to a boil, cover and simmer for 2–3 minutes until the mussels have opened.

Drain the mussels in a colander, then strain the stock into a clean pan. Remove the mussels from their shells, discarding any that remain closed.

Return the stock to a boil, add the milk, then stir in the cornstarch mixture to thicken. Add the herbs and season with black pepper.

Divide the mussels between 4 soup bowls and ladle the hot soup over them.

4 PORTIONS: 111 CALS, 9G PROTEIN, 5G FAT, 0.9G SATURATED FAT, 7G CARBOHYDRATE, 3.1G SUGAR, 0.9G FIBER, 195MG SODIUM

lentil, coconut and spinach soup

I love the earthiness of this soup. Any lentils could be used but I find the famous Puy lentils from France are as good as you can get and, for me, the best.

1 teaspoon cumin seeds
1 teaspoon cardamom seeds
1 tablespoon olive oil
1 onion, finely chopped
1 garlic clove, crushed
2 carrots, peeled and finely diced
6 ounces Puy lentils
1 quart vegetable stock (see page 156; if using
    packaged products or bouillon cubes use "low-salt" varieties)
½ cup reduced-fat coconut milk
handful of baby spinach leaves, stalks removed
freshly ground black pepper

Serves 4

Heat a dry non-stick pan. When hot, add the cumin and cardamom seeds and toast quickly for 30 seconds, moving them constantly in the pan.

Transfer the toasted seeds to a mortar and pestle (or spice grinder) and grind to a fine powder.

Heat the oil in a pan, add the vegetables and cook over a low heat with the ground spices for 4–5 minutes until the vegetables are lightly softened. Add the lentils and stock, bring to a boil and simmer for 20 minutes until the lentils are tender. Add the coconut milk for the last 5 minutes of cooking.

Just before serving, stir in the baby spinach leaves. Season to taste with black pepper and serve.

4 PORTIONS: 234 CALS, 13G PROTEIN, 8G FAT, 3.8G SATURATED FAT, 29G CARBOHYDRATE, 5.6G SUGAR, 5.5G FIBER, 99MG SODIUM

cantaloupe soup with lemongrass and mint

This is an adaptation of a recipe from my first book, *Virtually Vegetarian*, a refreshing chilled soup that will rely on the quality of your ripe melon. If orange-fleshed cantaloupes are not available, any type of melon can be substituted; watermelon makes a nice change.

1 ripe cantaloupe
juice of 2 limes
2 tablespoons dry sherry
1 tablespoon balsamic vinegar
2 teaspoons superfine sugar
4 stalks of lemongrass, outer husks removed,
    inner part finely chopped
8 fresh mint leaves

Serves 4

Cut the melon in half and remove the seeds, then cut away the skin and cut the flesh into large chunks.

Place in a blender with the lime juice, sherry, vinegar, sugar and lemongrass, along with ½ cup of cold water. Blend until smooth, then add half the mint leaves and blend again. Strain through a sieve into a bowl and chill for at least 4 hours, the longer the better.

To serve, shred the remaining mint leaves and add to the soup. Serve chilled.

4 PORTIONS: 50 CALS, 1G PROTEIN, 0G FAT, 0G SATURATED FAT, 11G CARBOHYDRATE, 9.8G SUGAR, 1.7G FIBER, 16MG SODIUM

spiced cashew nut and cauliflower soup

Cashew nuts are native to the north-east coast of Brazil, and have now spread to Vietnam, India and Africa. Like most nuts they are a source of fiber and protein and an excellent source of potassium, which can help lower blood pressure. However, due to their higher fat and calorie content, do not consume too many over a short period.

1 tablespoon olive oil
1 small onion, peeled and chopped
1 small head of cauliflower, cut into florets
1 medium potato, peeled and chopped
½ cup unsalted cashews
½ teaspoon ground cumin
pinch of ground turmeric
2½ cups vegetable stock (see page 156; if using
    packaged products or bouillon cubes
    use "low-salt" varieties)
½ cup 1% milk
freshly ground black pepper

Serves 4

Heat the oil in a heavy-bottomed saucepan, add the onions and cauliflower and cook for 6–8 minutes until vegetables have softened. Add the potatoes and cook for another 5 minutes.

Add the cashew nuts, cumin, turmeric and stock, bring to the boil, reduce the heat and simmer for 15–20 minutes until the vegetables are tender.

Add the milk, then transfer to a blender and process until smooth and creamy in texture. Season with black pepper and serve.

4 PORTIONS: 224 CALS, 11G PROTEIN, 14G FAT, 1.7G SATURATED FAT, 15G CARBOHYDRATE, 6.7G SUGAR, 3.4G FIBER, 52MG SODIUM

lima bean goulash soup

Although this soup is vegetarian-inspired, you can easily add a cup of lean ground beef to the vegetables, making it more hearty. I often like to serve this soup with some pieces of torn whole grain bread toasted until golden in the oven or under the broiler and drizzled with olive oil.

1 tablespoon olive oil
1 onion, peeled and chopped
2 carrots, peeled and cut into small dice
2 sticks celery, peeled and thinly sliced
1 garlic clove, crushed
1 teaspoon caraway seeds, coarsely crushed
1 tablespoon Hungarian sweet paprika
1 x 14½-ounce can no-added-salt tomatoes
1 tablespoon no-added-salt tomato paste
good pinch of sugar
11 ounces cooked lima beans
3 cups vegetable stock (see page 156; if using
    packaged products or bouillon cubes
    use "low-salt" varieties')
2 tablespoons chopped fresh flat-leaf parsley
freshly ground black pepper

Serves 4

Heat the olive oil in a heavy-bottomed saucepan. Add the onion, carrots, celery, garlic and caraway seeds and cook for 4–5 minutes until lightly softened but not golden. Add the paprika and cook for another 2 minutes.

Add the tomatoes, tomato paste and sugar, then add the lima beans. Pour in the stock, bring to a boil, reduce the heat and simmer for 20–25 minutes until the vegetables are tender. Add the chopped parsley, season to taste with black pepper and serve.

4 PORTIONS: 143 CALS, 8G PROTEIN, 4G FAT, 0.4G SATURATED FAT, 20G CARBOHYDRATE, 7.9G SUGAR, 5.7G FIBER, 104MG SODIUM

sweet potato, ginger and cinnamon soup

Rich in flavor, fiber, beta carotene and other key nutrients, sweet potatoes pack a real punch all around. This soup is a nice way to get your first taste if you haven't tried them before.

1 tablespoon olive oil
1 large onion, chopped
2 large orange-fleshed sweet potatoes,
   peeled and diced
1-inch piece ginger, peeled and finely chopped
1 quart vegetable stock (see page 156; if using
   packaged products or bouillon cubes
   use "low-salt" varieties)
½ cup cooked brown rice
1 teaspoon ground cinnamon
1 tablespoon chopped chives
freshly ground black pepper
crispy whole grain croutons (optional)

Serves 4

Heat the oil in a large saucepan, add the onion and cook gently for 5 minutes until it starts to soften.

Add the sweet potato, ginger and cinnamon and cook for another 5 minutes. Add the stock and cooked rice. Bring to a boil. Simmer for 30 minutes until the vegetables are soft and tender.

Transfer to a blender and process until smooth. Serve hot with the chopped chives and some crispy whole grain croutons, if desired.

4 PORTIONS: 221 CALS, 4G PROTEIN, 4G FAT, 0.7G SATURATED FAT, 45G CARBOHYDRATE, 11.6G SUGAR, 4.5G FIBER, 88MG SODIUM

thai-style shrimp broth

By using a good fresh fish stock you are guaranteed a lovely fragrant shrimp soup, full of vitality and freshness.

1 quart fish stock (see page 156; if using
   packaged products or bouillon cubes
   use "low-salt" varieties)
2-inch piece ginger, peeled and thinly sliced
1 red chile, very thinly sliced
2 stalks of lemongrass, outer husks removed,
   inside finely chopped
4 lime leaves, finely shredded
2 ounces baby spinach leaves
1 cup cooked rice noodles, broken into short lengths
4 scallions, shredded
handful of fresh cilantro leaves
8 ounces sustainably-sourced, cooked and peeled shrimp
freshly ground black pepper
juice of ½ lime

Serves 4

Bring the stock to a boil. Add the ginger, chile, lemongrass and lime leaves, reduce the heat and simmer for 15 minutes.

Add the spinach, noodles and scallions and simmer for another 5 minutes.

Finally add the cilantro and shrimp, season with black pepper and add the juice of the half lime. Serve immediately.

4 PORTIONS: 175 CALS, 16G PROTEIN, 1G FAT, 0.1G SATURATED FAT, 27G CARBOHYDRATE, 0.6G SUGAR, 0.4G FIBER, 443MG SODIUM

moroccan lamb broth (harira)

A classic Moroccan soup traditionally served to break the fast during Ramadan in many Middle Eastern countries. It can be a meal in itself, it is hearty and very tasty. Lemon is added at the end to give a characteristic tang to the soup.

½ pound lean diced leg of lamb, cut into ½-inch cubes
1 tablespoon olive oil
¼ teaspoon turmeric
½ teaspoon ground cinnamon
½ teaspoon ground ginger
2 onions, chopped
2 tablespoons chopped fresh cilantro
1 x 14½-ounce can no-added-salt diced tomatoes
1 teaspoon harissa (or 1 small red chile,
   de-seeded and finely chopped)
4½ ounces red lentils
4½ ounces cooked chickpeas (if canned, rinse
   under cold water)
2 ounces vermicelli noodles, broken into 1-inch lengths
1 egg, beaten with the juice of ¼ lemon
little extra lemon to serve (optional)

Serves 4

Place the lamb cubes in a saucepan, add the oil, spices, onions and cilantro and stir over low heat for 10 minutes, but do not brown.

Add the tomatoes and their juice along with the harissa or chile, then cover with 1½ quarts cold water. Bring to a boil, reduce the heat, add the lentils and simmer gently for 2 hours.

When ready to serve, add the cooked chickpeas and broken vermicelli and simmer for another 5 minutes.

Stir in the egg and lemon mix with a wooden spoon to create egg "strands". Season with black pepper and serve immediately with extra lemon, if desired.

4 PORTIONS: 392 CALS, 31G PROTEIN, 13G FAT, 4.1G SATURATED FAT,
41G CARBOHYDRATE, 6.7G SUGAR, 4.7G FIBER, 220MG SODIUM

zaalouk (moroccan eggplant)

Zaalouk is a traditional Moroccan salad made of eggplant, tomato and zucchini, cooked almost to a purée. It can be served hot or cold, eaten with a fork or as a dip. Traditionally it would be served with a Middle Eastern flatbread, but I also like to serve as a sort of Italian bruchetta on garlic-rubbed toast, which is equally delicious.

1 pound of eggplant, cut into 1-inch cubes
3 tablespoons olive oil
2 garlic cloves, crushed
1 red chile, deseeded and finely chopped
1 large zucchini, cut into 1-inch cubes
¼ teaspoon ground turmeric
½ teaspoon ground cumin
½ teaspoon paprika
10½ ounces plum tomatoes, cut into ½-inch cubes
3 tablespoons coarsely chopped fresh flat-leaf parsley
3 tablespoons coarsely chopped fresh cilantro
freshly ground black pepper
juice of ¼ lemon

Serves 4

Bring a pot of water to a boil, add the eggplant and simmer for 15 minutes, then drain then well and dry in a clean dishcloth.

Heat the olive oil in a large non-stick pan, add the garlic, chile and zucchini and cook over very low heat until the zucchini have softened. Add the cooked eggplant and spices and cook for another 5 minutes, then add the tomatoes. Continue to cook and mash the mixture with a spoon as it cooks into a coarse pulp.

When the mixture is well cooked, add the herbs, black pepper and lemon juice. Leave to cool—for best results, serve at room temperature.

4 PORTIONS: 122 CALS, 3G PROTEIN, 9G FAT, 1.2G SATURATED FAT,
7G CARBOHYDRATE, 5.6G SUGAR, 3.5G FIBER, 13MG SODIUM

roasted sweetcorn soup with chili popcorn

You will need fresh corn on the cob for this recipe —using the cobs helps to enhance the flavor of the base stock. Use unsalted popcorn.

2 large corn on the cob, in their husks
2 tablespoons olive oil
1 quart vegetable stock (see page 156; if using packaged products or bouillon cubes use "low-salt" varieties)
1 onion, peeled and chopped
white of 1 small leek, chopped
2 corn tortillas, cut into small pieces
½ cup 1% milk
freshly ground black pepper

For the chili popcorn
1 cup plain unsalted popcorn
pinch of chili powder
pinch of ground cumin

Serves 4

Preheat the oven to 375°F.

Place the corn in their husks into a roasting pan, drizzle with 1 tablespoon of the olive oil and place in the oven for 30 minutes, turning regularly until charred all over but not burnt. Remove from the oven, peel off the outer husks, then scrape off the kernels with a knife and reserve.

Cut the cobs into small pieces, place in a pot, cover with the stock and bring to a boil. Reduce the heat, simmer for 45 minutes, then strain, discarding the cobs.

Heat the remaining oil in a saucepan, add the onion and leek and cook over medium heat for 2–3 minutes. Add the chopped tortilla, stock and the corn kernels and bring to a boil. Simmer for 30 minutes. Transfer to a blender and process until smooth. Add the milk and season with black pepper. Keep hot.

For the popcorn, place in a bowl, add the chili powder and cumin and toss well. Serve the soup in hot bowls, topping each with a pile of chili-flavored popcorn.

4 PORTIONS: 402 CALS, 10.2G PROTEIN, 20.4G FAT, 2.7G SATURATED FAT, 47.3G CARBOHYDRATE, 6.6G SUGAR, 2.9G FIBER, 321MG SODIUM

crab salad "cocktail"

This dish is one of my favorite ways to enjoy fresh crab, bound in a fruity, low-fat crème fraîche with cilantro and juicy citrus fruits. I like to serve it in a martini-style glass, which makes for an elegant presentation. Try to buy fresh crabmeat if you can.

1 large orange
1 pink grapefruit
1 cup pineapple, cut into ½-inch cubes
½ cup golden raisins, soaked for 30 minutes
   in warm water, drained and dried
12 ounces fresh white crabmeat
juice of 2 limes
2 tablespoons maple syrup
1 teaspoon sherry vinegar
2 tablespoons reduced-fat crème fraîche
2 tablespoons chopped fresh cilantro
   (plus extra to garnish)
2 little gem (or baby) lettuce heads, leaves seperated, and shredded

Serves 4

Take the orange and grapefruit and peel them carefully, removing all the white pith. Using a sharp knife, cut between the membranes into neat segments, reserving the juices. Chop the segments into small dice.

Place the diced orange and grapefruit in a bowl and add the diced pineapple and raisins. Fold in the crabmeat and gently toss together.

In a separate bowl, whisk together the lime juice, maple syrup, vinegar and juices from the fruits. Add the crème fraîche and cilantro, season with black pepper and mix well. Add the dressing to the fruit and crabmeat, season with black pepper and combine well.

Arrange the shredded lettuce in the bottoms of 4 martini glasses, top with the crab mix, garnish with cilantro and serve.

4 PORTIONS: 176 CALS, 16G PROTEIN, 3G FAT, 0.9G SATURATED FAT,
23G CARBOHYDRATE, 22.8G SUGAR, 2G FIBER, 376MG SODIUM

cod and shellfish salad with roasted peppers

This makes a great first course or buffet salad. The seafood selection needs to be rinsed under a little cold running water to remove any excess salt.

½ cup fish stock (see page 156; if using packaged
   products or bouillon cubes use "low-salt" varieties)
1 bay leaf
1 pound sustainably-sourced skinless cod fillets
7 ounces roasted red peppers in oil, drained
2 garlic cloves, crushed
2 tablespoons roughly chopped fresh parsley
9 ounces assorted cooked seafood (shrimp, scallops
   mussels, squid), rinsed under cold water and dried
1 teaspoon sherry vinegar
juice of ½ lemon
3 tablespoons olive oil
freshly ground black pepper
pinch of smoked paprika
lemon wedges, to garnish

Serves 6

Heat the fish stock and bay leaf together in a small saucepan. Bring to a boil, then reduce the heat, add the cod and poach for 4–5 minutes until the fish is cooked and tender. Remove the fish from the liquid and set aside to cool.

Remove the bay leaf from the poaching liquid, return the liquid to a boil and reduce by half in volume. Transfer to a bowl and leave to cool.

Cut the peppers into strips and place in a bowl with the garlic, parsley, seafood, chilled reduced stock, sherry vinegar, lemon juice and olive oil. Mix well.

Flake in the poached cod fillet and season with ground black pepper and smoked paprika. Toss lightly to combine. Serve garnished with lemon wedges.

4 PORTIONS: 328 CALS, 34G PROTEIN, 17G FAT, 2.3G SATURATED FAT,
10G CARBOHYDRATE, 5.5G SUGAR, 4.4G FIBER, 1107MG SODIUM

beet, fennel and pomegranate salad

If you do not want to roast your own beets, you can use ready-cooked ones (but not pickled!). To remove the pomegranate seeds, scoop them into a bowl of water: the seeds will sink and the white pulp membranes will float.

1¼ pounds baby beets, with stalks attached if possible
2 tablespoons olive oil
2 heads of fennel, peeled and cut into wedges
2 heads Belgian endive (or chicory), leaves separated
9 ounces arugula leaves
2 tablespoons fresh flat-leaf parsley, leaves only
1 medium pomegranate, seeds removed and drained (see above)

For the dressing
1 tablespoon tahini
¹⁄₃ cup low-fat plain yogurt
1 teaspoon ground cumin
1 garlic clove, crushed
juice of 1 lemon
freshly ground black pepper

Serves 4

Preheat the oven to 350°F.

For the dressing, mix the tahini, yogurt, cumin and garlic in a bowl, stir in the lemon juice and season with black pepper. Set aside.

Trim the beets, leaving some of the stalks attached. Place on a sheet of foil, drizzle with the olive oil, add the fennel wedges, then scrunch up the foil to secure the vegetables within. Place on a baking sheet and roast for 1–1½ hours until tender. While warm, rub the skins off the beets and cut into small wedges.

Toss the endive, arugula and parsley leaves together and pile onto 4 serving plates. Top with the roasted beets and fennel, drizzle with the dressing, scatter the pomegranate seeds on top and serve.

4 PORTIONS: 220 CALS, 9G PROTEIN, 11G FAT, 1.6G SATURATED FAT, 22G CARBOHYDRATE, 18.1G SUGAR, 8.1G FIBER, 138MG SODIUM

roasted squash and coconut salad

The term summer and winter squashes can be confusing, as you tend to find one variety or another in the market all year. Butternut and pumpkin are probably the most common squash varieties, but you can use most varieties for this salad.

1 small butternut squash, peeled, deseeded and cut into large chunks
1 small pumpkin, peeled, deseeded and cut into large chunks
2 large zucchini, thickly sliced
1 tablespoon olive oil
freshly ground black pepper

For the dressing
1 teaspoon red Thai curry paste
½ cup reduced-fat coconut milk
juice of 2 limes
1-inch piece of ginger, peeled and grated
2 tablespoons chopped fresh cilantro
1 tablespoon chopped fresh mint

Serves 4

Preheat the oven to 400°F.

Place the squash and zucchini in a roasting pan, drizzle with a little olive oil and season with black pepper. Place in the oven and roast for 25–30 minutes or until the squash are tender and caramelized. Set aside to cool.

In a bowl, whisk together the ingredients for the dressing.

Place the caramelized squash in a bowl, pour the dressing over and toss together. Serve sprinkled with the peanuts.

4 PORTIONS: 194 CALS, 7G PROTEIN, 11G FAT, 4.5G SATURATED FAT, 19G CARBOHYDRATE, 11.6G SUGAR, 4.9G FIBER, 76MG SODIUM

peppered tuna, watermelon and grapefruit salad

It is vitally important that the tuna is extremely fresh for this dish, as it is served only seared on the exterior with the center still semi-raw. The fruit works extremely well with the tuna, making a wonderful salad to grace any table.

4 x 6-ounce very fresh, sustainably-sourced tuna fillets, cleaned thoroughly
4 tablespoons olive oil
4 teaspoons black peppercorns, cracked
1 cup peeled watermelon, cut into cubes
1 avocado, halved, pitted and sliced
1 grapefruit, peeled and cut into segments (reserve the juices)
3 scallions, finely shredded
1 red chile, deseeded and finely chopped
juice of 1 lemon
9 ounces mixed baby greens (try to include watercress)
cilantro for garnish (optional)

Serves 4

Preheat a grill or grill pan until almost smoking. Brush the tuna fillets with 1 tablespoon of the olive oil, then press each fillet into the cracked black peppercorns.

Place on the hot grill and cook for 30 seconds on each side to sear the exterior, then remove and set aside.

Place the watermelon, avocado, grapefruit segments and scallions in a bowl, add the chile, remaining oil and lemon juice and grapefruit juice. Toss together well, then add the salad leaves.

Cut each tuna fillet into 3 neat slices. Divide the salad between 4 serving plates, top with the peppered tuna, sprinkle over the cilantro, if using, and serve.

4 PORTIONS: 413 CALS, 38G PROTEIN, 25G FAT, 3.9G SATURATED FAT, 10G CARBOHYDRATE, 7.1G SUGAR, 2.5G FIBER, 79MG SODIUM

panzanella salad with grilled nectarines

Panzanella salad originates from Tuscany, and is often referred to as "leftover salad," as it contains a vast array of ingredients in its make-up. Traditionally the bread is soaked in the dressing, but I like the texture of toasted. This recipe also includes grilled nectarines, which when in season give the salad a juicy freshness.

4 firm but ripe nectarines, each pitted and cut into 6 wedges
4 tablespoons olive oil
freshly ground black pepper
10 ounces cherry tomatoes, halved
1 red onion, thinly sliced
2 ounces pitted green olives, rinsed under running water
4½ ounces reduced-fat mozzarella, cut into large cubes
10 ounces arugula leaves
20 small basil leaves (or basil cress)
1 tablespoon white balsamic vinegar (or white wine vinegar)
1 garlic clove, crushed
1 small white loaf of bread, cut into ½-inch cubes and toasted

Serves 4

Preheat a grill or grill pan until almost smoking. Brush the nectarine all over with 1 tablespoon of the olive oil, then place on the grill and cook for 4–5 minutes, turning regularly, until lightly charred all over. Remove, leave to cool and season with black pepper.

In a bowl, toss together the tomatoes, onion, green olives, mozzarella, arugula and basil.

Prepare a vinaigrette by whisking together the vinegar, remaining olive oil and garlic in a separate bowl. Season with black pepper. Add the vinaigrette to the tomatoes, toss together and add the toasted bread cubes. Leave to marinate for 20 minutes.

Divide the salad between 4 serving plates and top with the grilled nectarines.

4 PORTIONS: 485 CALS, 21G PROTEIN, 27G FAT, 9.9G SATURATED FAT, 43G CARBOHYDRATE, 17.1G SUGAR, 5G FIBER, 798MG SODIUM

punjabi chicken salad

This Indian Punjabi spiced chicken salad is low fat, the beet-yogurt dressing is wonderful and if you love Asian food this salad is sure to inspire.

4 x 6-ounce boneless and skinless
  chicken breasts
olive oil, for brushing
2 little gem (or baby) lettuces
7 ounces frisée lettuce
7 ounces cooked green beans
2 tablespoons chopped mint, plus
  leaves for garnish

For the marinade
juice of 1 lemon
$1/3$ cup low-fat plain yogurt
2 tablespoons chopped cilantro
1-inch piece ginger, peeled

2 garlic cloves, crushed
1 tablespoon garam masala
½ teaspoon cayenne pepper
1 tablespoon sunflower oil

For the dressing
1 large raw beet, peeled
  and cut into large chunks
$1/3$ cup low-fat plain yogurt
juice of ½ lemon
pinch of ground cumin
1 garlic clove, crushed

Serves 4

Place the chicken breasts in a non-reactive dish.

Mix the marinade ingredients in a bowl and pour over the chicken. Cover with plastic wrap and marinate in the fridge overnight.

Place the beets in a juicer, then place the juice in a small pan and reduce by half in volume until the juice becomes slightly syrupy in consistency. Remove to a bowl and leave to cool. When cold, add the yogurt, lemon juice, cumin and garlic, season with black pepper and set aside.

Heat a grill or grill pan, when hot, remove the chicken from the marinade, brush with oil and cook for 6–8 minutes until golden and lightly charred all over.

Place the lettuces, green beans and mint in a bowl, add some beet dressing and toss together. Arrange on 4 serving plates. Slice the grilled chicken and pile onto the salad. Sprinkle with mint leaves and serve.

4 PORTIONS: 289 CALS, 47G PROTEIN, 6G FAT, 1.3G SATURATED FAT, 11G CARBOHYDRATE, 8.2G SUGAR, 3.3G FIBER, 209MG SODIUM

lemon quinoa tabbouleh with grilled vegetables

Nutty-tasting quinoa (pronounced keen-wah) makes a nice alternative to the traditional cracked wheat in this recipe.

6 ounces quinoa
1½ cups boiling water
2 small eggplants, thickly sliced
2 zucchini, thickly sliced
1 red pepper, deseeded, quartered and cut into large cubes
1 yellow pepper, deseeded, quartered and cut into large cubes
1 head fennel, cut into 1-inch thick slices

Serves 4

2 tablespoons olive oil
freshly ground black pepper
zest and juice of 2 lemons
2 tablespoons superfine capers, rinsed and dried
2 ounces walnut halves, chopped
12 mint leaves, roughly chopped
2 tablespoons roughly chopped, fresh flat-leaf parsley

Place the quinoa in a pan, pour in the boiling water, cover, reduce the heat and cook for about 20 minutes until the grains are tender. Drain in a colander, transfer to a bowl and leave to cool.

Liberally brush the eggplant, zucchini, peppers and fennel with the olive oil and season with black pepper.

Preheat a grill or grill pan and, when very hot, add the vegetables and grill until cooked and lightly charred (you may need to do this in batches). When all the vegetables are cooked, add to the cooked quinoa.

Add the lemon juice and zest, capers, walnuts and chopped herbs to the quinoa. Mix together well, adjust seasoning and serve.

4 PORTIONS: 330 CALS 12G PROTEIN, 17G FAT, 1.7G SATURATED FAT, 34G CARBOHYDRATE, 11.4G SUGAR, 5.5G FIBER, 191MG SODIUM

smoked chicken tortilla salad

This salad is a solid favorite ever since the day my good friend Dean Fearing, then the Chef of The Mansion on Turtle Creek in Texas, first prepared it for me. Here is my adaptation on the same idea.

1 carrot, peeled and finely chopped
1 red pepper, deseeded and finely chopped
1 green pepper, deseeded and finely chopped
1 yellow pepper, deseeded and finely chopped
2 tablespoons sunflower oil
2 corn tortillas
handful of fresh cilantro leaves
8 ounces sweet corn kernels (canned without salt is fine, rinse under cold water and dry)
7 ounces cooked black beans
14 ounces sliced, smoked chicken, cut into strips

For the dressing
handful of fresh cilantro leaves
1 shallot, chopped
1 red chile, deseeded and chopped
2 tablespoons honey
juice of 4 limes

Serves 4

For the dressing, place the cilantro, shallot and red chile in a blender with 1 cup water and process into a purée. Stir in the honey and lime juice.

Place the carrot and peppers in a bowl, add the dressing and toss well together. Set aside for 20 minutes for the vegetables to soften in the dressing.

Heat the oil in a non-stick saute pan. When hot add the corn tortillas and fry until crisp and golden all over, about one minute on each side. Remove the tortillas and dry on paper towels. Allow to cool.

Break up the tortillas into small pieces and quickly toss with the vegetables. Add the cilantro, sweet corn, black beans and chicken and toss again. Pile high on serving plates.

4 PORTIONS: 437 CALS, 27G PROTEIN, 19G FAT, 4.5G SATURATED FAT, 43G CARBOHYDRATE, 14.7G SUGAR, 6.2G FIBER, 1182MG SODIUM

spanish roasted tomato salad

In this recipe oven-roasted tomatoes are dressed in sherry vinegar, then delicately seasoned with cumin and herbs. This salad is best made in the height of the summer when naturally sweet tomatoes and crisp fava beans are at their best.

12 medium ripe, firm plum tomatoes, cut in half lengthwise
1 garlic clove, crushed
2 teaspoons superfine sugar
freshly ground black pepper
pinch of ground cumin
3 tablespoons olive oil
10 ounces fava beans in their pods
2 tablespoons coarsely chopped fresh mint
4 scallions, finely chopped
2 hard-boiled eggs, peeled and chopped

For the dressing
1 garlic clove, crushed
1 red chile, deseeded and finely chopped
¼ teaspoon ground cumin
4 tablespoons olive oil
2 teaspoons sherry vinegar
¼ teaspoon Spanish paprika

Serves 4

Preheat the oven to 150°F.

Place the tomatoes on a baking sheet, then sprinkle with garlic, sugar, black pepper and cumin. Drizzle with the olive oil. Place in the oven for 1 hour until the tomatoes have started to curl up at the edges and look shrivelled. Leave to cool. This can be done several hours ahead.

Pod the fava beans and cook in boiling water for 3 minutes, then drain and rinse under cold water. Dry in a cloth and remove the tough outer skins.

For the dressing, mix together the ingredients in a bowl. In a separate bowl, add the fava beans, mint and scallions to the tomatoes, then add enough dressing to taste.

Place on a serving plates, sprinkle with the chopped egg and serve.

4 PORTIONS: 318 CALS, 10G PROTEIN, 24G FAT, 3.7G SATURATED FAT, 16G CARBOHYDRATE, 11.2G SUGAR, 6.9G FIBER, 68MG SODIUM

chapter three

starters & light dishes

crab cakes with shrimp and harissa-mango salsa

Making cakes from pounded meat or seafood has been a tradition in many countries; they are easy to make and very tasty—and my recipe is no exception.

1 tablespoon sunflower oil
watercress leaves, to garnish
12 large, sustainably-sourced shrimp,
   peeled, deveined and cooked

For the crab cakes
1 pound fresh white crabmeat
1/3 cup whole grain breadcrumbs
1 teaspoon ground cumin
¼ teaspoon ground turmeric
¼ teaspoon paprika
4 tablespoons reduced-fat mayonnaise
2 tablespoons chopped cilantro
½ teaspoon dried chile flakes
juice of ½ lemon

For the mango salsa
1 red pepper, deseeded and cut
  into small dice
1 small mango, peeled and cut
  into small dice
2 tablespoons chopped fresh cilantro
2 tablespoons maple syrup
¼ teaspoon harissa, or 1 small red chili,
  finely chopped
1-inch piece ginger, peeled and grated
juice of 2 limes

Serves 6

For the crab cakes, mix all the ingredients in a bowl. Season with black pepper and refrigerate for up to 4 hours to firm up the mix.

Divide the crab mix into 6 equal-size round patties, approximately 3 inches in diameter, and return to the fridge.

For the salsa, place all the ingredients in a bowl and season to taste with black pepper. Leave to infuse for 1 hour before serving.

To serve, heat the oil in a large non-stick pan, add the crab cakes, and cook for 3–4 minutes on each side.

Place the crab cakes on serving plates, top each with 2 shrimp and top with some of the salsa. Garnish with the watercress and serve.

6 PORTIONS: 228 CALS, 23.5G PROTEIN, 7G FAT, 1G SATURATED FAT, 18.9G CARBOHYDRATE, 10.9G SUGAR, 2.2G FIBER, 696MG SODIUM

parsley risotto with lemon and shrimp

The intense flavor of the parsley really works well with this risotto and the vibrant color is visually amazing.

1 cup fresh flat-leaf parsley, washed
1 tablespoon olive oil
2 shallots, finely chopped
10½ ounces risotto-style rice (e.g. arborio)
1 quart vegetable stock (see page 156; if using packaged products or bouillon cubes use "low-salt" varieties)
2 pounds sustainably-sourced jumbo shrimp, shelled, deveined and each cut into large pieces
zest and juice of ¼ lemon
2 tablespoons dry white wine
freshly ground black pepper

Serves 4

Place the parsley into a small pan of boiling water, blanch for 1 minute then drain. Place the parsley in a small blender with ⅓ cup of the vegetable stock, process to a purée and set aside.

Heat the olive oil in a heavy-bottomed saucepan, add the shallots, cover and cook over a low heat until softened. Add the rice and cook for 1 minute until the rice becomes translucent. Add the white wine and cook for 1 minute.

Meanwhile bring the remaining stock to a boil in a different pan. Add a little of this stock to the rice and cook until the liquid has been absorbed before adding more. Continue this way until the rice has absorbed all the stock and is tender but still retaining a little bite (al dente).

Add the shrimp, parsley purée, lemon zest and cook for 2 minutes. Season with black pepper. Divide between 4 bowls and serve.

4 PORTIONS: 377 CALS, 27G PROTEIN, 5G FAT, 0.7G SATURATED FAT, 60G CARBOHYDRATE, 1.1G SUGAR, 2.8G FIBER, 254MG SODIUM

grilled sardines with thai relish

Fresh sardines are now more widely available. Here they are grilled in a Thai-spiced coating and served with a refreshing style relish.

12–16 fresh sardines, cleaned
2 garlic cloves, crushed
½ teaspoon dried red chilli flakes
1-inch piece ginger, grated
juice of 1 lime
2 tablespoons olive oil
pinch of sugar

For the relish
juice of 2 limes
3 ounces unsalted roasted peanuts, chopped
1 red chili, finely chopped
1 tablespoon sweet chile sauce
2 tablespoons chopped fresh cilantro
1 small red pepper, deseeded and finely chopped

Serves 4

Slash the flesh of the sardines 2–3 times on each side.

Mix the garlic, chili flakes, ginger, lime juice, oil and sugar in a bowl, then rub the mixture all over the sardines to coat thoroughly. Set aside for 1 hour to infuse the flavors.

For the relish, mix all the ingredients together in a bowl.

Preheat the grill or grill pan until almost smoking. Place the sardines on the grill and cook for 2–3 minutes on each side until cooked through. Top with the relish and serve immediately.

4 PORTIONS: 442 CALS, 37G PROTEIN, 29G FAT, 5.5G SATURATED FAT, 8G CARBOHYDRATE, 5.5G SUGAR, 1.5G FIBER, 247MG SODIUM

mackerel with white navy bean and horseradish aioli

It can be difficult to obtain fresh horseradish in many stores and supermarkets so I have succumbed to use the creamy version that is more readily available. However, these can be high in sodium so check the label. You can prepare your own roasted red peppers if you prefer, but there are some good jarred varieties out there now.

1 teaspoon Dijon mustard
juice of ¼ lemon
3 tablespoons olive oil
1 pound cooked white navy beans, hot
2 roasted red peppers, skinned and cut into small dice
1 red onion, thinly sliced
¾ pound new potatoes, cooked, peeled and sliced
freshly ground black pepper
4 x 4-ounce sustainably-sourced fresh mackerel fillets, boneless
good handful of arugula leaves
lemon wedges, to garnish

For the aioli
$1/3$ cup reduced-fat mayonnaise
1 tablespoon creamed horseradish
1 garlic clove, crushed

Serves 4

First off prepare a lemon vinaigrette by whisking together the mustard, lemon juice and 2 tablespoons of the olive oil. Add the hot beans, roasted peppers, onion and potatoes and season with black pepper. Keep warm.

Heat a non-stick pan with the remaining olive oil, season the mackerel fillets with black pepper and cook, skin-side down for 2–3 minutes until the skin becomes crispy, then turn over and cook for another 2 minutes.

Mix together the ingredients for the aioli and season with black pepper.

Arrange the arugula leaves on serving plates and top with the mackerel fillets. Place a little spoonful of aioli to one side and serve.

4 PORTIONS: 645 CALS, 33.8G PROTEIN, 40.6G FAT, 6.7G SATURATED FAT, 38.6G CARBOHYDRATE, 8G SUGAR, 11.9G FIBER, 837MG SODIUM

marinaded salmon with pear and fennel

This recipe makes a wonderful starter for a special occasion. The fresh salmon fillets are cooked in a warm bath of olive oil infused with black pepper, star anise and fresh vanilla, which gives it a delicate flavor and an almost uncooked appearance.

1 vanilla pod (or ½ teaspoon vanilla extract)
1½ cups extra virgin olive oil
1 teaspoon cracked black peppercorns
3 star anise pods
4 x 6-ounce very fresh, sustainably-sourced salmon fillets, skinless, boneless
1 large head fennel, fronds removed, peeled and halved
juice of one lemon
2 tablespoons coarsely chopped dill
4 tablespoons olive oil
2 small, firm, but ripe pears, cored and cut in half

Serves 4

Take the vanilla pod and split it lengthways. Using a small knife, scrape out the inner black seeds into a bowl. Chop up the pod itself and place in a shallow saucepan with the olive oil. Add the peppercorns and star anise and bring the oil to a light simmer for 2 minutes, then remove from the heat and leave the flavors to infuse the oil. Strain the oil and return it back to the pan, using a thermometer to heat it to 130°F.

Keeping the temperature constant, cook the salmon fillets for 12–15 minutes until cooked through (the appearance will be very opaque as it is cooked at such a low temperature). Transfer the salmon to a plate, pat dry with paper towels to absorb the excess oil and allow to cool.

Using a mandoline, slice the fennel halves wafer thin, then add to the bowl with the vanilla seeds. Add the lemon juice, dill and olive oil. Slice the pears thinly and add to the fennel. Season with black pepper and toss together.

Place the salmon fillets on 4 individual serving plates, top with fennel and pear and garnish with more dill. Serve at room temperature.

4 PORTIONS: 633 CALS, 31.3G PROTEIN, 53.4G FAT, 8.5G SATURATED FAT, 7.4G CARBOHYDRATE, 6.6G SUGAR, 2.7G FIBER, 77MG SODIUM

whole grain spaghetti with sardines and raisins

In this recipe I have combined a Venetian speciality "Sarde in Saor" or soused sardines, mixed with spaghetti with added raisins to give a little sweetness. It works really well together.

12 fresh sardines, filleted and bones removed
a little whole grain flour
2 tablespoons olive oil
1 small onion, thinly sliced
2 teaspoons superfine sugar
¼ cup white wine vinegar
pinch of saffron powder
4 tablespoons dry white wine
1 pound whole grain spaghetti
1½ ounces raisins, soaked in warm water for
    30 minutes and drained
3 tablespoons pine nuts, lightly toasted

Serves 4

Lightly dredge the sardine fillets in a little whole grain flour. Heat 1 tablespoon of the olive oil in a non-stick pan, add the sardine fillets and cook for 30 seconds on each side until golden. Remove and drain on paper towels.

Return the pan to the heat and add the remaining oil. Add the onion and sugar and cook for 5–6 minutes until golden. Add the vinegar, then the saffron and white wine and cook for 2–3 minutes. Remove from the pan and set aside.

Lay the sardine fillets in a dish, layered with the onions. Leave for 2 hours before use.

Cook the spaghetti in a large pot of boiling water until al dente, then drain in a colander. Return to the pot, add the sardines and onion, then the raisins and pine nuts. Toss together, season with black pepper and serve.

4 PORTIONS: 795 CALS, 51G PROTEIN, 29G FAT, 4.9G SATURATED FAT, 87G CARBOHYDRATE, 15.2G SUGAR, 10.2G FIBER, 355MG SODIUM

mussel bouillabaise

I adore mussels prepared any style, but this one is very French in its make-up. The sauce has a warming glow about it and an aniseed flavor. Top with the garlic toasted slices of French bread for the perfect accoutrement.

1 tablespoon olive oil
1 onion, finely chopped
1 garlic clove, crushed
1 small bulb fennel, peeled and finely chopped
1 x 14½-ounce can diced tomatoes (no added salt)
½ teaspoon fresh thyme leaves
1 small bay leaf
juice and zest of ½ orange
2½ cups fish stock (see page 156; if using packaged stock
    or bouillon cubes use "low salt" varieties)
pinch of saffron
3 tablespoons Pernod
2+ pounds cleaned mussels
1 tablespoon chopped fresh flat-leaf parsley
4 slices baguette, toasted and rubbed with
    garlic and olive oil (optional)

Serves 4

Heat the olive oil in a large saucepan. Add the onion, garlic and fennel and cook for 10–12 minutes until the vegetables are soft and just starting to color.

Add the tomatoes, thyme, bay leaf, orange zest and juice and cook for 5 minutes.

Pour in the fish stock, saffron and Pernod and bring to a boil. Throw in the cleaned mussels, cover with a lid and cook for 3–4 minutes until the mussels have opened. Discard any that remain closed. Transfer to serving dishes, pour over the cooking sauce, sprinkle over the chopped parsley and serve with the toasted baguette.

4 PORTIONS: 199 CALS, 14G PROTEIN, 5G FAT, 0.7G SATURATED FAT, 20G CARBOHYDRATE, 5.9G SUGAR, 2.9G FIBER, 414MG SODIUM

pasta with duck ragu, orange and sage gremolata

With its rustic texture, whole grain pasta stands up well to bold, earthy sauces.

1 pound dried whole grain noodles (tagliatelle or penne)

For the duck ragu
3 tablespoons olive oil
4 fresh duck legs, skin removed
freshly ground black pepper
1 onion, peeled and chopped
1 carrot, peeled and chopped
2 garlic cloves, crushed
4 sage leaves, chopped
1/3 cup red wine

1 cup chicken stock (see page 156; if using packaged stock or cubes use "low salt" varieties)
7 ounces canned, diced tomatoes
2 tablespoons freshly grated parmesan

For the gremolata
4 sage leaves, finely chopped
zest of 1 orange
1/2 garlic clove, crushed
2 tablespoons olive oil

Serves 6

First make the duck ragu. Heat the oil in a heavy-bottomed flameproof casserole dish or pan. Season the duck legs with black pepper and add to the pan, turning them until colored all over. Transfer to a plate. Add the onions, carrot and garlic to the pan juices and cook until lightly golden. Add the wine, stock and tomatoes and bring to a boil. Add the sage and reduce to a simmer. Cover with a lid and simmer for 1 hour.

Transfer the duck to a plate and allow to cool, remove the meat from the bones, then return the meat to the sauce, cook for a further 10 minutes. Season and keep warm.

For the gremolata, toss all the ingredients together in a bowl. Cook the pasta in boiling water until just al dente, then drain in a colander.

To serve, stir the duck ragu sauce into the pasta, then divide between 4 serving bowls. Sprinkle with a little parmesan, then the orange-sage gremolata.

4 PORTIONS: 242 CALS, 20G PROTEIN, 17G FAT, 2.8G SATURATED FAT, 4G CARBOHYDRATE, 1.2G SUGAR, 0.1G FIBER, 422MG SODIUM

tunisian chicken liver kebabs with lemon mayonnaise

A wonderful and exotic addition to your barbecue repetoire.

20 fresh (or frozen) chicken livers (about 1 pound), any green bile removed
1 tablespoon olive oil
1 teaspoon ground cumin
1 teaspoon smoked paprika
2 tablespoons white wine vinegar
freshly ground black pepper

For the lemon mayonnaise
1/2 cup reduced-fat mayonnaise
zest and juice of 1 lemon
2 scallions, very finely chopped
1 tablespoon chopped fresh cilantro

Serves 4

Dry the chicken livers with paper towels to remove excess moisture. In a bowl combine the oil, spices and vinegar. Add the chicken livers and leave to marinate for 1 hour. Soak 4 wooden skewers in water.

Carefully thread 5 chicken livers onto each skewer. Brush with the marinade.

Heat a grill or grill pan until very hot, add the skewers and cook for 3–4 minutes on each side until cooked and lightly charred all over.

Mix the ingredients for the lemon mayonnaise in a bowl and season with black pepper.

Serve the kebabs and mayonnaise with a crisp green salad and warm pita bread wedges.

4 PORTIONS: 242 CALS, 20G PROTEIN, 17G FAT, 2.8G SATURATED FAT, 4G CARBOHYDRATE, 1.2G SUGAR, 0.1G FIBER, 422MG SODIUM

portobello mushrooms al forno

"Al forno" is an Italian culinary term describing food that is baked or passed through an oven.

8 large portobello mushrooms, stalks
   removed and reserved
2 teaspoons olive oil
1 onion, finely chopped
7 ounces cooked, chopped spinach leaves
3 ounces sun-dried tomatoes (not in oil), chopped
6 ounces reduced-fat mozzarella, cut into small cubes
1 egg yolk
freshly ground black pepper
2 ounces whole grain breadcrumbs
2 tablespoons prepared pesto

Serves 4

Preheat oven to 400°F.

Chop the mushroom stalks finely. Heat half the olive oil in a non-stick pan, add the onion and chopped mushroom stalks and cook over low heat until softened.

Add the spinach and sun-dried tomatoes and mix well. Transfer to a bowl and set aside until cool.

Add the mozzarella, mix well, then stir in the egg yolk. Season with black pepper.

Brush the mushroom cups liberally with the remaining olive oil, then fill each with the mushroom-onion filling. Place the stuffed mushrooms in a single layer in an ovenproof dish.

In a bowl, mix the breadcrumbs, the remaining olive oil and the pesto, then sprinkle liberally over the mushrooms. Bake for 8–10 minutes until tender with a lightly golden crust.

4 PORTIONS: 236 CALS, 18.3G PROTEIN, 12.1G FAT, 4.4G SATURATED FAT, 14.3G CARBOHYDRATE, 5.1G SUGAR, 4.3G FIBER, 370MG SODIUM

goan egg curry with tofu and chickpeas

Being a great lover of eggs, I adore this curry made with eggs, chickpeas and firm tofu; it makes a lovely vegetarian dish. Serve with steamed basmati rice. Tamarind paste often contains salt, so check the label.

1 tablespoon sunflower oil
1 onion, thinly sliced
11 ounces firm tofu, cut into ½-inch cubes
½ teaspoon red chile powder
¼ teaspoon ground turmeric
1 teaspoon ground coriander
¼ teaspoon ground cumin
 2 good handfuls of delicate baby spinach,
   stalks removed
2 tablespoons chopped fresh cilantro
4 plum tomatoes, cut into ½-inch cubes
1¼ cups reduced-fat coconut milk
1 tablespoon tamarind paste
6 freshly cooked hard-boiled eggs
   (I recommend 8 minutes), peeled
5 ounces cooked chickpeas

Serves 4

Heat the oil in a saucepan, add the onion and cook for 5 minutes until softened. Add the tofu and cook for 2 minutes. Add the spices and cook over a gentle heat for another 5 minutes.

Add the baby spinach and cilantro and cook until it wilts down, about 2 minutes. Add the tomatoes, coconut milk and tamarind paste, simmer gently for another 5 minutes.

Cut the hard-boiled eggs in half and add to the curry along with the chickpeas. Season with black pepper and gently heat through. Serve with the steamed rice.

4 PORTIONS: 385 CALS, 21.7G PROTEIN, 26.0G FAT, 12.4G SATURATED FAT, 17.9G CARBOHYDRATE, 8.5G SUGAR, 4.1G FIBER, 325MG SODIUM

chapter four

main courses

gnocchi with pumpkin, mushrooms and parsley

The Italians waste nothing, and from nothing create wonderful dishes of sheer brilliance. Here, stale whole grain breadcrumbs are transformed into light, fluffy dumplings—a great vegetarian dish.

2¼ cups whole grain flour
3½ ounces whole grain breadcrumbs
1 tablespoon freshly grated Parmesan
2 tablespoons olive oil
½ small pumpkin, skinned, deseeded and diced

10½ ounces cremini mushrooms, thinly sliced
2 garlic cloves, crushed
2 tablespoons roughly chopped fresh parsley
freshly ground black pepper
ground nutmeg

Serves 4

In a bowl, mix the flour with the breadcrumbs and add enough warm water to form a thick but soft elastic dough. Add the Parmesan and turn out the dough onto a floured work surface. Knead the dough for 4–5 minutes until soft.

Roll out the dough into 1-inch thick ropes, then cut these into 1-inch pieces. Roll each piece into a ball and then press them with your thumb and shape them into small gnocchi.

Bring a large pot of water to a boil, add the gnocchi and simmer for 15–20 minutes—they will float to the surface of the pan. Remove with a slotted spoon and drain.

Meanwhile, heat the olive oil in a non-stick pan, add the pumpkin and cook for 4–5 minutes over medium heat until it softens. Add the mushrooms and garlic and cook for about 5 minutes until golden. Add the parsley and the drained gnocchi to the pan and toss well. Season with black pepper and nutmeg and serve in pasta-style bowls.

4 PORTIONS: 524 CALS, 21G PROTEIN, 10G FAT, 1.8G SATURATED FAT, 93G CARBOHYDRATE, 4.9G SUGAR, 14.3G FIBER, 84MG SODIUM

grilled tandoori vegetables

In the summer these vegetables are excellent cooked on an outdoor barbecue. Serve with a classic mint-flavored yogurt sauce on the side.

1 teaspoon ground cumin
1 teaspoon garam masala
1 teaspoon ground coriander
¼ teaspoon ground turmeric
½ teaspoon red chile powder
2 garlic cloves, crushed
juice of 1 lemon
little red food coloring (optional)
½ cup low-fat plain yogurt
4 small onions, peeled, halved
1 celery root, peeled and cut into large pieces.

1 small butternut squash, peeled and cut into wedges
14 ounces baby carrots, peeled
8 baby eggplants, halved
1 large red pepper, deseeded and cut into thick strips
2 tablespoons olive oil
lemon wedges, to serve
⅓ cup low-fat plain yogurt
2 tablespoons chopped fresh mint, to serve

Serves 4

Place the spices, garlic, lemon juice and food coloring, if using, into a bowl and mix into a paste with the yogurt.

Blanch the onions and celery root in a pan of boiling water for 5 minutes, then refresh under cold water, drain well and dry. Stir into the yogurt marinade along with the remaining vegetables, rubbing the marinade well into the vegetables. Cover with plastic wrap and refrigerate for 24 hours (48 hours is even better) to allow the flavors to infuse.

Heat a grill or grill pan. When hot, remove the vegetables from the marinade, brush with the oil, place on the grill and cook, turning regularly to ensure even cooking and charring —it will take 20–25 minutes until the vegetables are soft and cooked through.

Combine yogurt and mint to create a sauce. Serve with the lemon wedges.

4 PORTIONS: 254 CALS, 10G PROTEIN, 9G FAT, 1.2G SATURATED FAT, 35G CARBOHYDRATE, 25.1G SUGAR, 13.2G FIBER, 242MG SODIUM

split pea and apricot vadas

The great thing about these little vadas is that they can be prepared in advance and frozen. Vadas are a type of savory snack from southern India. They can vary in both shape and size, though generally they are prepared in a disc shape. Made from various legumes mixed with gram (chickpea) flour, they are commonly prepared in Indian homes or sold as a snack food throughout the Indian sub-continent. Gram flour is available from health food stores. Serve with tamarind chutney.

8 ounces yellow split peas, soaked overnight in lots of water
3 ounces dried apricots, soaked in warm water, drained and dried
2 tablespoons gram flour
1 teaspoon cumin seeds, lightly toasted
½ teaspoon curry powder
½ teaspoon fennel seeds, lightly toasted
1 small green chile, deseeded and finely chopped
1 small onion, finely chopped
sunflower oil, for frying
¹/₃ cup low-fat plain yogurt, to serve
tamarind chutney, to serve

Serves 4

Place the split peas and apricots in a blender, process in quick pulses until the mix is coarsely ground. Transfer to a bowl, add the gram flour, spices, chile and onion and combine well. Place in refrigerator to chill for 30 minutes.

Using wet hands, divide the mixture into 24 equal-size balls, then flatten them slightly.

Heat a deep sided non-stick pan with 1 inch of sunflower oil. When hot add the vadas, a few at a time, and cook until golden and crispy. Drain on paper towels.

Place the vadas on a serving plate, drizzle with yogurt, then drizzle with the tamarind chutney. Serve.

4 PORTIONS: 293 CALS, 15G PROTEIN, 7G FAT, 1.3G SATURATED FAT, 45G CARBOHYDRATE, 10.2G SUGAR, 5.8G FIBER, 39MG SODIUM

summer provençale bake

A simple Provençal-inspired bake or gratin, great as a vegetarian main course or as a vegetable to accompany a meat or fish dish. If you like you can add some reduced-fat mozzarella to the vegetables before sprinkling over the crust.

1 red onion, peeled and cut into wedges
4 medium zucchini, thickly sliced
2 eggplants, cut into 1-inch cubes
2 heads of fennel, trimmed, fronds removed and cut into wedges
9 ounces sundried tomatoes in oil
2 garlic cloves, crushed
freshly ground black pepper
3½ ounces whole grain breadcrumbs
1 tablespoon prepared pesto
1 tablespoon chopped fresh flat-leaf parsley

Serves 4

Preheat the oven to 400°F.

Place onion, zucchini, eggplant, fennel, sundried tomatoes and their oil in a bowl, add the garlic and season with black pepper.

Arrange in a gratin dish large enough to hold all the vegetables in a single layer. Place in the oven and bake for 30 minutes, basting regularly with juices until the vegetables are golden.

In a separate bowl, mix the crumbs, pesto and parsley. Spoon the crumb mix over the vegetables and return the dish to the oven for 5 minutes until the crust is golden.

4 PORTIONS: 435 CALS, 10G PROTEIN, 34G FAT, 4.9G SATURATED FAT, 24G CARBOHYDRATE, 10.8G SUGAR, 7.9G FIBER, 690MG SODIUM

caraway roasted vegetables with chestnut polenta

This is a dish I love to serve at Christmas, served with cranberry sauce on the side. The vegetables can be changed to your preference. Some brands of polenta contain salt so always check the label.

2 red onions, quartered
4 carrots, halved lengthways
4 parsnips, thinly sliced diagonally
10 ounces Brussels sprouts, halved
3 tablespoons olive oil
freshly ground black pepper
1 teaspoon caraway seeds

For the polenta
3½ ounces precooked, vacuum-packed chestnuts
2 cups 1% milk
1 garlic clove, crushed
2 sprigs thyme
4½ ounces instant polenta
pinch of grated nutmeg
freshly ground black pepper

Serves 4

Preheat the oven to 400°F.

Place the vegetables in a roasting pan, drizzle with 2 tablespoons olive oil, season with black pepper and caraway and toss together. Roast the vegetables for 45 minutes or until tender and caramelized. Meanwhile, place the chestnuts in a blender with a little water and process into a wet paste.

Bring the milk, garlic and thyme to a boil and simmer for 5 minutes, then remove the thyme sprigs.

Sprinkle in the polenta a little at a time, whisking constantly at first and then using a wooden spoon as it thickens. Add the chestnut purée and season with nutmeg and black pepper. The polenta should be the consistency of wet mashed potato, slightly pourable.

Divide the polenta between 4 serving plates, top with the vegetables, drizzle with the remaining olive oil and serve.

4 PORTIONS: 459 CALS, 14G PROTEIN, 15G FAT, 3G SATURATED FAT, 71G CARBOHYDRATE, 29.5G SUGAR, 13.5G FIBER, 108MG SODIUM

sweet and sour squid with cucumber and yogurt rice

Give me squid, squid and more squid, I love it! This dish is a solid favorite in our home. Crab would be lovely the same way.

1⅓ pounds cleaned squid, including tentacles
½ teaspoon mild curry powder
½ teaspoon ground coriander
1 tablespoon sunflower oil
1 garlic clove, crushed
4 scallions, coarsely chopped
2 tablespoons rice wine vinegar
1 tablespoon mango chutney (finely chopped)
2 tablespoons sweet chile sauce

1½ ounces raisins, soaked for 30 minutes, drained and dried
1 tablespoon chopped fresh mint
1 tablespoon chopped fresh cilantro
¼ cucumber, peeled, halved and thickly sliced
juice of 2 limes
10 ounces basmati rice, cooked
3 tablespoons low-fat plain yogurt
freshly ground black pepper
lime wedges, to garnish

Serves 4

Cut the squid into ½-inch thick pieces lengthways. Place in a bowl and rub with the curry powder and ground coriander. Set aside.

Heat the oil in a non-stick wok or pan, add the squid, garlic and scallions and quickly stir-fry for 1 minute. Transfer to a plate.

Add the vinegar, chutney, sweet chili sauce, raisins and herbs to the pan and cook over high heat for 1 minute. Return the squid to the sauce, add the cucumber and lime juice and combine together.

Add the yogurt to the hot basmati rice and season with the black pepper.

Arrange the yogurt rice on serving plates, top with the squid and garnish with the lime wedges.

4 PORTIONS: 474 CALS, 32G PROTEIN, 6G FAT, 0.5G SATURATED FAT, 77G CARBOHYDRATE, 14.4G SUGAR, 1.8G FIBER, 376MG SODIUM

grilled salmon with mixed peas and watercress

This dish is perfect for an outdoor summer lunch. Lots of varying textures and extremely delicate in flavor. It is nice to garnish the dish with pea tendrils if available and some nice steamed new potatoes. If you prefer the peas can be steamed instead of boiled.

4 x 6 ounces sustainably-sourced, skinless and boneless salmon fillets
3 tablespoons olive oil
freshly ground black pepper
10 ounces snow peas, ends cut off and strings removed
10 ounces sugar snap peas
9 ounces fresh peas (podded weight) or use frozen

1 garlic clove, crushed
juice of ½ lemon
3½ ounces sundried tomatoes in oil, drained and coarsely chopped
1 teaspoon cracked coriander seeds
2 tablespoons roughly chopped fresh cilantro
bunch of watercress
fresh pea tendrils, to garnish

Serves 4

Preheat a grill or grill pan. Brush the salmon lightly with 1 tablespoon of the olive oil and season with black pepper. Place on the grill and cook for 2–3 minutes on each side.

Meanwhile, blanch the snow peas, sugar snap peas and fresh peas in a pan containing a little boiling water for 1 minute. Drain well and season with black pepper.

Heat the remaining oil in a pan with the garlic, lemon juice, tomatoes, coriander seeds and fresh cilantro. Heat gently for 5 minutes to infuse the flavor.

To serve, divide the peas between 4 plates, top each with a grilled salmon fillet, spoon a little of the tomato dressing over the top and garnish with watercress and pea tendrils, if available. Serve immediately.

4 PORTIONS: 509 CALS, 46G PROTEIN, 29G FAT, 5.4G SATURATED FAT, 16G CARBOHYDRATE, 8.5G SUGAR, 6.7G FIBER, 102MG SODIUM

catalan tuna steaks

Tuna is very popular in Spain, but especially revered in Catalonia. Here the fish is topped with "samfaina", a sort of Spanish ratatouille that makes a perfect pairing with the richness of the oily tuna. The samfaina is finished with a spicy dressing, which adds a lovely bite to the sauce. I like to serve this with hot, steamed new potatoes on the side.

4 x 6-ounce sustainably-sourced fresh tuna steaks
freshly ground black pepper
2 tablespoons olive oil
1 onion, cut into a large dice
2 garlic cloves, crushed
2 green peppers, halved, deseeded and cut lengthways into strips
1 red pepper, halved, deseeded and cut lengthways into strips
good pinch of saffron

4 firm ripe tomatoes, cut into a large dice
1 zucchini, cut into large dice
1 teaspoon superfine sugar

For the spiced dressing
1 tablespoon sherry vinegar
1 teaspoon paprika
¼ teaspoon red chili flakes (or harissa)
1 tablespoon olive oil

Serves 4

Season the tuna steaks with black pepper. In a large non-stick pan, heat half the olive oil, add the tuna and cook for 1 minute on each side. Transfer to a plate and keep warm.

Add the remaining oil to the pan, add the onion, garlic and peppers and cook for 5 minutes until they begin to soften. Add the saffron, diced tomatoes, zucchini, sugar and ½ cup of water.

Return to a boil, add the tuna steaks, cover and simmer gently over very low heat for 2–3 minutes.

Mix the ingredients for the dressing together and stir into the cooking sauce. Transfer to a platter and serve immediately.

4 PORTIONS: 381 CALS, 45G PROTEIN, 17G FAT, 3.1G SATURATED FAT, 11G CARBOHYDRATE, 9.5G SUGAR, 3.2G FIBER, 99MG SODIUM

baked hake with peas, lettuce and clams

A dish I love to prepare—simple and tasty. Mussels can be used instead of clams, following the same method. This is also good served with mashed potatoes, whipped until light and fluffy with a little good olive oil.

4 eggs
2 tablespoons olive oil
1 onion, finely chopped
2 garlic cloves, crushed
4 x 7-ounce sustainably -sourced hake steaks
1½ pounds small vongole-style fresh clams
4 ounces fresh peas (podded weight, or use frozen)

1 head gem (baby) lettuce, shredded
3 tablespoons roughly chopped fresh flat-leaf parsley
½ cup dry white wine
⅓ cup fish stock (see page 156; if using packaged products or bouillon cubes use "low-salt" varieties)

Serves 4

Preheat the oven to 375°F.

Bring a small pan of water to a boil, carefully immerse the eggs into the pan and simmer gently for 5 minutes until soft boiled. Remove, peel and keep warm.

Meanwhile heat the olive oil in an ovenproof casserole dish on top of the stove, add the onion and garlic and cook for 1–2 minutes. Place the pieces of hake on top and cook for 1–2 minutes on each side until golden.

Add the clams, peas, lettuce, parsley, white wine and stock and bring to a boil. Cover and place in the oven to braise for 6–8 minutes or until tender.

Arrange the hake on individual serving plates, then top with the clams and braising liquid. Cut each egg in half and use to decorate the dish. Serve immediately.

4 PORTIONS: 401 CALS, 50G PROTEIN, 18G FAT, 3.7G SATURATED FAT, 8G CARBOHYDRATE, 4.1G SUGAR, 2.2G FIBER, 307MG SODIUM

baked trout with sorrel and blueberries

The tart flavor of the sorrel works beautifully in this dish with the sweet-tasting blueberries. I serve the trout with steamed young baby carrots.

4 x 8-ounce sustainably-sourced fresh trout, gutted and cleaned
2 tablespoons sorrel, leaves only
2 tablespoons fresh flat-leaf parsley
6 ounces blueberries
1 garlic clove, crushed
1 tablespoon balsamic vinegar
½ teaspoon Dijon mustard
freshly ground black pepper

Serves 4

Preheat the oven to 375°F.

With a sharp knife remove the head from the fish. Slash the fish three times on each side. Place it skin side up on a work surface and gently press down on the backbone to loosen it from the fish. Flip over and ease the backbone away from the fish with your hands.

Carefully remove as many of the inner small bones as possible, then bring the halves of the fish back together to form its original shape. Place the sorrel and remaining ingredients (except the blueberries) in a blender and process into a smooth, thick sauce. Season the trout with black pepper.

Place the trout in a large, lightly greased baking dish, open them up, divide the sorrel sauce between them and fold back together to conceal the sauce. Neatly return them to their original shape and scatter the blueberries on top.

Cover the fish with foil and bake for 15 minutes, then uncover and cook for another 10 minutes until the trout is cooked.

Carefully remove the fish using a long spatula and place on individual serving plates. Spoon any excess pan juice over the fish and serve with steamed carrots, if desired.

4 PORTIONS: 324 CALS, 44G PROTEIN, 14G FAT, 2.9G SATURATED FAT, 5G CARBOHYDRATE, 3.9G SUGAR, 1.2G FIBER, 149MG SODIUM

snapper in crazy water

A strange-sounding dish, first created by Neapolitan fishermen in Italy who cooked the fish in "Aqua Pazza" or "crazy water". I have tasted numerous variations: here is mine. For a tasty alternative, add some small clams or mussels to the broth along with the fish. Try serving the snapper on a bed of lightly sautéed spinach and cooked chickpeas in olive oil.

2 tablespoons olive oil
¼ teaspoon red chili flakes
2 small bay leaves
2 garlic cloves, peeled and thinly sliced
4 tablespoons dry white wine
1 lemon, thinly sliced
1 dried anchovy fillet, soaked in water for 10 minutes, then chopped
2 tablespoons superfine baby capers, rinsed, drained
10 ounces ripe firm tomatoes, chopped
4 x 6-ounce sustainably-sourced snapper fillets, cleaned
freshly ground black pepper
3 tablespoons roughly chopped fresh flat-leaf parsley

Serves 4

Place the olive oil, chili flakes, bay leaves and garlic in a shallow sauce pan, cover with the wine and 1½ cups of water and bring to a boil. Add the lemon slices, anchovy, capers and tomatoes, then reduce the heat to a simmer.

Season the fish with black pepper, then add it to the broth along with the parsley—the liquid should come only halfway up the fish. Cover with a lid, reduce the heat and poach the snapper for 3–4 minutes until just tender.

Transfer the fish to deep serving bowls, spoon some of the broth over the top and garnish to serve.

4 PORTIONS: 239 CALS, 35.7G PROTEIN, 8.3G FAT, 1.3G SATURATED FAT, 4.6G CARBOHYDRATE, 4.1G SUGAR, 1.2G FIBER, 339MG SODIUM

porgy with kumquats and artichokes

This dish is an adaptation of a similar dish I had in Paris at one of France's best-known haunts, Le Bouquinistes. If kumquats are not available, orange segments or slices would work equally well.

3 tablespoons olive oil
1 pound large new potatoes, cleaned and cut in half lengthwise
freshly ground black pepper
10 ounces cooked artichoke hearts
2 tablespoons chopped fresh cilantro
2 tablespoons pine nuts, toasted
4 x 6-ounce cleaned sustainably-sourced porgy fillets
1 shallot, peeled, finely chopped
4½ ounces kumquats, sliced
4 tablespoon dry white wine
¾ cup chicken stock (see page 156; if using packaged products or bouillon cubes use "low-salt" varieties)
1 tablespoon balsamic vinegar
freshly ground black pepper

Serves 4

Preheat the oven to 375°F.

Heat half the olive oil in a baking pan, add the potatoes, toss well and season with black pepper. Cook in the oven for 30–40 minutes until golden, turning often. Add the artichokes during the last 10 minutes of the cooking time. Remove from the oven, add the cilantro and pine nuts and keep warm.

Heat the remaining oil in a non-stick pan. Season the fish with black pepper and cook until crispy, about 2 minutes per side. Remove the fish from the pan and keep warm.

Add the shallot and kumquats to the pan and cook over low heat until they are just beginning to brown slightly. Add the white wine, chicken stock and vinegar and boil for 3–4 minutes or until the sauce has reduced in volume by one third.

Arrange the vegetables on serving plates, top each with a porgy fillet, drizzle with a little sauce, then serve.

4 PORTIONS: 414 CALS, 35G PROTEIN, 17G FAT, 2.5G SATURATED FAT, 30G CARBOHYDRATE, 6.1G SUGAR, 4.6G FIBER, 220MG SODIUM

grilled tuna with butternut squash, caramelized onion and mint vinaigrette

A great dish for a summer barbecue, the vinaigrette can be made well in advance and the rest put together very quickly. I often serve this with some steamed couscous or new potatoes. Asparagus, in common with other vegetables, is a good source of potassium, which can help lower blood pressure.

1 butternut squash
16 asparagus stalks, trimmed
1 tablespoon olive oil
1 garlic clove, crushed
1 red chile, deseeded and finely chopped
4 x 6-ounce sustainably sourced tuna steaks
freshly ground black pepper

For the vinaigrette
3 tablespoons olive oil
2 small red onions, finely chopped
1 tablespoon honey
2 tablespoons balsamic vinegar
2 tablespoons chopped fresh mint
freshly ground black pepper

Serves 4

Cut the butternut squash into 12 wedges, discard the inner seeds and, using a small knife, remove the outer skin.

Cook the asparagus in a pan of boiling water for 2–3 minutes, then remove with a slotted spoon and set aside.

For the vinaigrette, heat 1 tablespoon of the olive oil in a pan, add the onions and cook for 4–5 minutes until lightly browned and softened. Add the honey and caramelize gently in the pan for another 15 minutes. Remove from heat and allow to cool. Add the balsamic vinegar, remaining oil and chopped mint, season with black pepper and set aside.

Preheat a grill or grill pan until hot. Toss the butternut squash wedges and asparagus with a little oil, garlic and chile and place the squash on the grill to cook for 10–12 minutes, then add the asparagus, cook for another 5 minutes, or until the vegetables are golden and lightly caramelized. Remove and keep warm.

Season the tuna steaks then brush with a little olive oil. Place on the grill for 2–3 minutes until the tuna is cooked rare (a little longer if you prefer it more well done).

Place the tuna steaks on a bed of the grilled squash and asparagus, spoon the onion and mint vinaigrette over the top and serve.

4 PORTIONS: 407 CALS, 44G PROTEIN, 19G FAT, 3.4G SATURATED FAT, 15G CARBOHYDRATE, 10.1G SUGAR, 2.5G FIBER, 89MG SODIUM

fish couscous

Couscous is the national dish of Morocco. It is a semolina grain, so it is a starchy food that provides energy, fiber, vitamins and minerals. It can be served with meat or vegetables cooked in a spicy broth. This is a recipe I like to make at home, conjuring up many wonderful memories of a trip to Marrakech, such an enticing and mystical city. Serve the couscous with a selection of roasted vegetables of your choice, prepared with a touch of olive oil and seasoned with ground cumin.

4 x 6 ounce boneless sustainably-sourced
 sea trout fillets or other flaky white fish
selection of vegetables for roasting,
 e.g. ½ pound carrots, ½ pound squash, and
 2 zucchini, cut in large, equal-size pieces
dash of olive oil
16 ounces quick-cook couscous
1¾ cups boiling water or chicken stock
½ teaspoon dried chili flakes
2 tablespoons sunflower oil

For the marinade
1 garlic clove, crushed
2 tablespoons chopped fresh cilantro
 (plus a few extra leaves to garnish)
2 tablespoons chopped fresh flat-leaf parsley
3 tablespoons olive oil
½ teaspoon ground cumin
½ teaspoon sweet paprika
¼ teaspoon cayenne pepper
¼ teaspoon ground turmeric
juice of 1 small lemon
½ cup chicken stock (see page 156; if using
 packaged products or bouillon cubes use
 "low-salt" varieties)

Serves 4

In a dish combine all the marinade ingredients except the chicken stock. Add the fish fillets to the marinade. Cover with plastic wrap and keep in the fridge overnight.

Preheat the oven to 400°F and roast the carrots and squash pieces in a little olive oil for 25 minutes. Add the zucchini and cook for another 10 minutes until all are cooked and golden.

Place the couscous in a bowl, add the boiling water, chili flakes and oil and combine well. Cover with plastic wrap and set aside for 5 minutes to steam. Remove the plastic wrap and fluff the couscous with a fork. Cover with plastic wrap again and leave to steam for another 2 minutes. Keep warm.

Remove the fish from the marinade, place in a baking pan and bake for 6–8 minutes or until cooked.

Meanwhile, heat the stock in a saucepan, whisk in the marinade ingredients and bring to a boil.

Pile the couscous high on serving plates. Top with the roasted vegetables, then the fish fillets. Drizzle with some of the marinade broth, garnish with the extra cilantro and serve.

4 PORTIONS: 600 CALS, 42G PROTEIN, 22G FAT, 3.7G SATURATED FAT, 62G CARBOHYDRATE, 4G SUGAR, 1G FIBER, 122MG SODIUM

baked cod boulangère

The beauty of this dish is that the cod fillets release their juices into the potatoes when they are baked—quite delicious. Boulangère potatoes are so named because in France they were given to local bakers to place in their bread ovens after the day's baking to cook slowly.

3 tablespoons olive oil, for greasing and drizzling
2¼ pounds potatoes, peeled and thinly sliced
2 onions, thinly sliced
freshly ground black pepper
1 teaspoon chopped fresh rosemary
13 ounces hot chicken stock (see page 156; if using packaged products or bouillon cubes use "low-salt" varieties)

4 x 6-ounce sustainably sourced cod fillets, skin on
2 tablespoons olive oil
8 ounces chanterelle mushrooms
2 tablespoons roughly chopped fresh flat-leaf parsley

Serves 4

Preheat the oven to 350°F.

Lightly grease a large ovenproof dish with a little olive oil. Arrange layers of the potatoes and onions in the dish, seasoning each layer with black pepper and a little rosemary.

Finish with a layer of the potatoes in an overlapping pattern. Press down on the potatoes firmly. Pour the hot stock on top of the potatoes, enough to just cover. Cover with tin foil and cook in the oven for 40 minutes. Remove the foil and return to the oven to brown the potatoes for another 20 minutes.

Season the cod with black pepper. Place the cod fillets on top of the potatoes, drizzle each with a little olive oil and return the dish to the oven for 10–12 minutes to cook the fish.

To finish, heat the remaining oil in a non-stick pan, when hot add the mushrooms and cook for 2–3 minutes until golden. Season, add the flat-leaf parsley and mix well.

Arrange the cod and boulangère potatoes on serving plates. Spoon the mushrooms over the top and serve.

4 PORTIONS: 480 CALS, 39G PROTEIN, 16G FAT, 2.3G SATURATED FAT, 48G CARBOHYDRATE, 4.5G SUGAR, 4.7G FIBER, 135MG SODIUM

grilled porgy with cauliflower and caper sauce

The caper sauce adds a wonderful piquant flavor to the porgy, and is also great served over scallops and grilled vegetables. Make it a day ahead, it will help the flavors meld together beautifully.

2 tablespoons olive oil
1 garlic clove, crushed
½ red chile, deseeded and finely chopped
1 pound cauliflower florets
good pinch of saffron
2 tablespoons pine nuts, toasted
2 ounces raisins, soaked in warm water for 30 minutes, drained and dried
freshly ground black pepper
4 x 6-ounce sustainably-sourced porgy fillets, boneless

For the sauce
2 tablespoons capers, rinsed
1 tablespoon chopped tarragon
1 tablespoon chopped flat-leaf parsley
1 small roasted red pepper, cut into small dice
1 shallot, finely chopped
1 hard-boiled egg, peeled and chopped into small pieces
3 tablespoons olive oil
juice of ½ lemon

Serves 4

Heat 1 tablespoon of the olive oil in a non-stick pan, add the garlic, chile and cauliflower and cook for 2 minutes. Add a little water and the saffron and cook gently until the cauliflower is cooked but still retaining its shape. Add the pine nuts and raisins and season with black pepper.

Heat a grill or grill pan until hot. Season the fish fillets with black pepper, brush with oil then cook, skin-side down, for 3–4 minutes, then carefully turn them over using a spatula and cook for another 2–3 minutes or until cooked.

Meanwhile, mix together all the ingredients for the sauce in a bowl and season with black pepper.

Arrange the cauliflower on 4 serving plates, top each with a grilled fish fillet, spoon the caper sauce over and serve.

4 PORTIONS: 424 CALS, 38G PROTEIN, 25G FAT, 3.7G SATURATED FAT, 14G CARBOHYDRATE, 12.3G SUGAR, 3G FIBER, 465MG SODIUM

monkfish with beets, cumin and braised lentils

I love to serve this on creamy olive oil mashed potatoes or a parsnip mash, both are delicious.

10 ounces raw beets, peeled and cut into 1-inch cubes
2 tablespoons olive oil
2 shallots, finely chopped
½ teaspoon ground cumin
1 garlic clove, crushed
6 ounces Puy lentils (or Castelluccio)
1½ cups chicken stock
(see page 156; if using packaged products or bouillon cubes use "low-salt" varieties)
few sprigs of thyme

2 tablespoons balsamic vinegar
1 teaspoon superfine sugar
freshly ground black pepper
4 x 6-ounce cleaned sustainably sourced monkfish fillets, each cut into 3 equal-sized pieces
2 tablespoons sunflower oil
2 tablespoons chopped cilantro

For the shallot purée
6 large shallots, thinly sliced
1 cup 1% milk
2 ounces short-grain rice

Serves 4

Cover the beets with water in a pot and cook for 50 minutes–1 hour until tender. Heat the olive oil in a heavy-bottomed pan, add the shallots, cumin and garlic and cook together for 1 minute. Add the lentils, chicken stock and thyme, bring to a boil and simmer for 30 minutes. Heat the vinegar and sugar in a separate pan, add the beets and lightly cook for 2–3 minutes until they develop a sweet and sour flavor.

When the lentils are cooked, stir in the sweet and sour beets, season with black pepper and keep warm.

For the purée, blanch the shallots in a pan of boiling water for 5 minutes, then drain. Return to the pan, add the milk and rice, bring to a boil and simmer for 30 minutes. Transfer to a blender and process until smooth.

Season the monkfish with black pepper. Heat the oil in a non-stick pan, add the monkfish and cook for 3–4 minutes on each side until golden and cooked through. Arrange the fish on 4 individual serving plates, garnish with the beets, lentils, shallot purée and cilantro and serve immediately.

4 PORTIONS: 458 CALS, 41G PROTEIN, 14G FAT, 2.4G SATURATED FAT, 44G CARBOHYDRATE, 12.3G SUGAR, 5.8G FIBER, 139MG SODIUM

roasted skate with fruit and vegetable sauce

Skate has to be very fresh to enjoy it at its best: as a rule I like to consume it within eight hours of purchasing, as old skate can release an ammonia like smell and flavor which is very unpleasant. When fresh it can be a revelation.

1 Granny Smith apple, peeled and cored
1 small mango, peeled
5½ ounces fresh pineapple
1 small red pepper, halved and deseeded
2 celery stalks, trimmed
freshly ground black pepper
2 tablespoons canola oil
4 x 10-ounce sustainably-sourced skate wings

juice of 1 lemon
2 tablespoons sherry vinegar
2 teaspoons brown sugar
⅓ cup tomato juice (no added salt)
1 tablespoon baby capers, rinsed and drained
2 tablespoons chopped fresh flat-leaf parsley
3 cups spinach, to serve

Serves 4

Cut the apple, mango and pineapple into small dice. Cut the celery and red pepper to the same size and set aside.

Heat 1 tablespoon of the oil in a large non-stick pan. Season the skate wings with black pepper and lemon juice and add to the pan. Cook the skate over medium heat for 3–4 minutes each side until crisp and golden. When cooked, transfer to a plate and keep warm.

Return the pan to the heat, add the prepared fruit and vegetables and cook for 2 minutes. Add the sherry vinegar, sugar and tomato juice and simmer for 1 minute. Finally add the capers and parsley and season with black pepper.

Steam the spinach for 2 minutes and season with black pepper. Arrange on a plate, place the skate on top, spoon the sauce over the fish and serve.

4 PORTIONS: 267 CALS, 32G PROTEIN, 7G FAT, 0.5G SATURATED FAT, 21G CARBOHYDRATE, 20.1G SUGAR, 3.5G FIBER, 402MG SODIUM

cioppino (seafood stew)

Often spelled "Ciuppin", this seafood stew is said to have originated in the waters off San Francisco. The word ciuppin means chopped in Italian and it is said the fishermen made the stew on board their vessels while at sea, using chopped fish.

2 tablespoons olive oil
1 head fennel, thinly sliced
1 onion, chopped
1 garlic clove, crushed
½ teaspoon red chili flakes
1¼ pounds mixed fish (e.g. snapper, halibut), cut into large pieces
4 tablespoons dry white wine
1 cup fish stock (see page 156; if using packaged products or bouillon cubes use "low-salt" varieties)
1 x 14½-ounce can diced tomatoes (no added salt)
12 raw shrimp, peeled and deveined
3 tablespoon Pernod
2 tablespoons chopped fresh flat-leaf parsley

Serves 4

In a shallow heavy-bottomed pan, heat the oil, add the fennel, onion and garlic and cook over low heat for 8–10 minutes until softened and lightly caramelized.

Add the chili flakes and fish pieces on top of the fennel. Pour in the wine and boil for 1 minute. Add the fish stock and tomatoes and bring to a simmer. Add the shrimp and Pernod and simmer for another 5 minutes. Stir in the parsley and serve immediately.

4 PORTIONS: 343 CALS, 37G PROTEIN, 15G FAT, 2.6G SATURATED FAT, 7G CARBOHYDRATE, 5.1G SUGAR, 2.7G FIBER, 284MG SODIUM

grilled sea bass with lemongrass and ginger pesto

An asian twist on the Italian classic "pesto" sauce. I serve the bass on grilled slices of zucchini but asparagus is also good with the dish. Marinating fish in lime or lemon juice before cooking helps avoid the need to add salt for flavor.

4 x 6-ounce cleaned
   sustainably-sourced sea
   bass fillets
freshly ground black pepper
juice of 1 lime
2 tablespoons olive oil
14 ounces zucchini, sliced
   thickly on the bias

For the pesto
2 lemongrass stalks, outer
   husks removed, insides very
   finely chopped
2-inch piece ginger, peeled
   and finely chopped
1 garlic clove, crushed
15 fresh basil leaves
small bunch fresh cilantro leaves
1 ounce unsalted roasted peanuts
4 tablespoons sunflower oil

Serves 4

Place the sea bass in a shallow dish, season with black pepper, pour in the lime juice with the olive oil and leave to marinate for 1 hour at room temperature.

To cook the zucchini, heat a grill pan until very hot. Season the thick-cut slices of zucchini with black pepper and grill for 4–5 minutes, turning them regularly until cooked and golden.

For the pesto, place all the ingredients in a small blender and process into a coarse purée. Heat a grill or grill pan, add the sea bass fillets and cook for 3–4 minutes, skin-side down, until golden and crispy. Carefully turn over and cook for another 2 minutes.

Arrange the sea bass fillets on a bed of grilled zucchini slices and top with the asian pesto sauce.

4 PORTIONS: 337 CALS, 38G PROTEIN, 19G FAT, 3G SATURATED FAT, 4G CARBOHYDRATE, 2.3G SUGAR, 1.3G FIBER, 124MG SODIUM

fish curry

Traditionally, when I make a chicken-style curry, I always use coconut milk. However, in this variation that uses fish I prefer to use yogurt, making the sauce a little more tart and also lower in saturated fat. Most types of fish work well here; salmon, halibut or cod. Serve with hot basmati rice—a simple but impressive dish.

2-inch piece ginger, peeled
4 garlic cloves
½ cup low-fat plain yogurt
1 tablespoon white flour
2¼ pounds sustainably-sourced
   firm white fish fillets, cut
   into 2-inch cubes
4 tablespoons sunflower oil
2 onions, chopped
½ teaspoon ground turmeric

½ teaspoon red chile powder
1 tablespoon ground coriander
1 tablespoon ground cumin
6 whole cardamom pods, crushed
2-inch stick of cinnamon
1 teaspoon sugar
2 ounces ground almonds
2 tablespoons chopped cilantro
   to garnish

Serves 4

Place the ginger and garlic in a blender, add 4 tablespoons water and process into a smooth paste. In a bowl, mix together the yogurt and flour, then stir in the ginger paste. Add the fish, cover with plastic wrap and refrigerate for 1 hour.

Heat the oil in a heavy-bottomed non-stick pan, add the onions and cook until lightly golden. Add the spices and cook gently for another 3–4 minutes.

Remove the fish from the fridge, and add both the fish and the marinade to the pan with the onions. Increase the heat, add 1 cup of water and carefully bring to a boil. Add the sugar and almonds, reduce the heat and cook gently for 10–12 minutes, stirring occasionally.

Transfer to a serving plate, sprinkle with the cilantro to garnish and serve with basmati rice.

4 PORTIONS: 463 CALS, 53G PROTEIN, 22G FAT, 2.6G SATURATED FAT, 15G CARBOHYDRATE, 7G SUGAR, 1.9G FIBER, 196MG SODIUM

vietnamese-style snapper

Vietnam is a wonderful haven of great culture and food, which is always light, fragrant and clean tasting. This dish is no exception, embodying the virtues of quick, simple and delicious. Perfect for either a simple family meal or a dinner party main course. Lovely served with some steamed or stir-fried Asian greens.

4 x 6-ounce sustainably-sourced snapper fillets, cleaned, boneless
1 tablespoon sunflower oil
1 teaspoon sesame oil
2 garlic cloves, crushed
juice of 2 limes
2 lemongrass stalks, outer leaves removed, tender insides chopped
1 red chile, finely sliced
1 tablespoon rice wine vinegar
2 tablespoons sweet chile sauce

½ cup chicken stock (see page 156; if using packaged products or bouillon cubes use "low-salt" varieties)
1 teaspoon reduced-salt soy sauce
2 red peppers, deseeded and cut lengthways into strips
1 red onion, thinly sliced
4 scallions, thickly sliced on bias
3 tablespoons roughly chopped fresh cilantro

Serves 4

Place the snapper fillets in a shallow dish, pour in both oils, add the garlic, lime juice, lemongrass and chile and rub well into the fish. Cover with plastic wrap and leave to marinate for 1 hour at room temperature.

Heat the vinegar and sweet chile sauce in a large, deep-sided non-stick pan. When hot, add the chicken stock, soy sauce, peppers, onion, scallions and cilantro, reduce the heat and cook for 5 minutes.

Add the marinated snapper fillets to the pan and spoon the sauce over them. Cover the pan with a lid and simmer for 4–5 minutes, basting the fish occasionally with the sauce.

To serve, arrange the fish on serving plates, top with the braising sauce and garnish with a little cilantro and lime.

4 PORTIONS: 250 CALS, 36.1G PROTEIN, 6.5G FAT, 1G SATURATED FAT, 12.6G CARBOHYDRATE, 11G SUGAR, 1.8G FIBER, 327MG SODIUM

braised chicken in vinegar sauce

A lovely way to enjoy chicken, slowly braised in a sauce made from cider vinegar, delicately flavored with Dijon mustard.

8 chicken thighs, skin removed
freshly ground black pepper
2 tablespoons sunflower oil
4 garlic cloves, crushed
3 shallots, peeled and finely chopped
½ cup cider vinegar (or white wine vinegar)
2 tablespoons honey
⅓ cup dry white wine
⅔ cup chicken stock (see
    page 156; if using packaged products or
    bouillon cubes use "low-salt" varieties)
2 teaspoons "salt free" tomato paste
1 teaspoon Dijon mustard
1 tablespoon chopped tarragon

Serves 4

Season the chicken thighs with black pepper. Heat the sunflower oil in a heavy-bottomed pan, add the chicken pieces and cook for 5–6 minutes until golden, turning regularly. Transfer to a plate.

Remove any excess fat from the pan, add the garlic and shallots and cook for 2–3 minutes until softened. Add the vinegar, honey and white wine and reduce in volume by half. Add the stock, bring to a boil, return the chicken to the pan and cook for 10–15 minutes.

Mix the tomato paste with the Dijon mustard and then stir into the sauce. When the chicken is cooked, add the tarragon and season with black pepper. The sauce should be slightly tart in flavor, if necessary add a tablespoon more vinegar, then serve.

4 PORTIONS: 318 CALS, 37G PROTEIN, 10G FAT, 2.5G SATURATED FAT, 12G CARBOHYDRATE, 11.1G SUGAR, 0.3G FIBER, 214MG SODIUM

baby chicken spatchcock with lemon and herbs

This is a lovely way to cook these tender young chickens. Ask your butcher to butterfly or "spatchcock" them. That means the backbone and breast bones are removed to give a toad like appearance. The flavoring of the lemon and herbs with the delicate meat is magical. Sweet and sour root vegetables are my preferred way to serve them.

1 garlic clove, crushed
2 tablespoons chopped fresh mixed herbs
  (i.e. thyme, rosemary, flat-leaf parsley)
½ lemon
4 baby chickens (1 pound each) butterflied or
  spatchcocked, skin removed
freshly ground black pepper
2 tablespoons olive oil
11 ounces young carrots, peeled
11 ounces young parsnips, peeled and halved
  lengthways
1 tablespoon olive oil
1 tablespoon maple syrup
2 tablespoons chopped fresh mint
1 tablespoon balsamic vinegar
⅔ cup chicken stock (see page 156;
  if using packaged products or bouillon
  cubes use "low-salt" varieties)

Serves 4

Preheat the oven to 400°F.

In a bowl, mix the garlic and herbs. Cut one half of the lemon into thin slices.

Lay the chickens out on a large baking pan and season with pepper. Using a small sharp knife, make small incisions over the chickens, then rub the garlic and herb mix into the slots. Place a slice or two of lemon on each chicken and drizzle with the olive oil. Roast for 18–20 minutes until chicken is cooked through.

Meanwhile, blanch the carrots and parsnips in boiling water for 2 minutes, then drain. Place them in a separate baking pan, drizzle with olive oil and maple syrup and roast until golden and lightly caramelized, about 20 minutes. Towards the end of the cooking, add the mint and balsamic vinegar and season. Keep hot.

When the chicken is cooked, remove from the baking pan and set aside. Add the stock to the pan, place over high heat and deglaze, scraping up in any bits that have caramelized on the bottom. Boil for 2 minutes and season with pepper.

Place the roasted vegetables on serving plates, top each with a roasted spatchcock chicken, spoon the pan juices over the plates and serve.

4 PORTIONS: 374 CALS, 46G PROTEIN, 14G FAT, 2.5G SATURATED FAT, 18G CARBOHYDRATE, 11.7G SUGAR, 5.3G FIBER, 198MG SODIUM

hazelnut chicken with leeks and mushroom vinaigrette

If wild mushrooms are not available, portobellos make a good alternative.

1 egg
4 x 6-ounce skinless chicken
   breasts, bone in
2½ ounces ground hazelnuts
2 tablespoons sunflower oil
14 ounces leeks, washed and
   roughly shredded

For the vinaigrette
1 tablespoon sunflower oil
11 ounces wild mushrooms, cleaned

1 shallot, finely chopped
1 tablespoon sherry vinegar
⅓ cup chicken stock
   (see page 156; if using
   packaged products or
   bouillon cubes use "low-salt"
   varieties)
2 tablespoons hazelnut oil
1 tablespoon olive oil
1 tablespoon chopped
   flat-leaf parsley
freshly ground black pepper

Serves 4

Beat the egg with 1 tablespoon water in a shallow dish. Dip the chicken breasts in the egg mixture, then dredge in the ground hazelnuts. Be sure to coat the breasts well.

Heat 1 tablespoon of the oil in a non-stick pan, add the leeks and 1/3 cup water, cover, reduce the heat and cook for 8–10 minutes until the leeks are tender. Drain and keep warm.

Return the pan to the heat and add another 1 tablespoon of the oil. When hot, add the chicken breasts and cook for 4–5 minutes on each side until the chicken is cooked and the nutty coating is golden.

For the vinaigrette, heat another small non-stick pan. When hot add the sunflower oil, mushrooms and shallot and cook for 1–2 minutes until golden. Add the vinegar and stock and boil for 2 minutes. Stir in the hazelnut and olive oils, add the parsley and season with black pepper.

Arrange the leeks on serving plates, pour on some of the mushroom vinaigrette, top with a nut-coated cooked chicken breast and serve.

4 PORTIONS: 491 CALS, 49G PROTEIN, 30G FAT, 3.7G SATURATED FAT, 5G CARBOHYDRATE, 3.1G SUGAR, 3.8G FIBER, 158MG SODIUM

braised chicken with squash, saffron and mint

A simple dish I often like to prepare at home with a Moroccan feel and delicate flavor. Always buy the best quality olives available within your price range with the least amount of salt, I find many are over salted and lack any real flavor.

2½ cups chicken stock (see page
   156; if using packaged
   products or bouillon cubes use
   "low-salt" varieties)
good pinch of fresh saffron
   (or powdered)
12 chicken thighs, skins removed
freshly ground black pepper
1 tablespoon whole grain flour
2 tablespoons olive oil

1 small butternut squash,
   peeled and cubed
12 ounces baby onions, peeled
1 lemon, thinly sliced
1 garlic clove, crushed
2 teaspoons honey
12 pitted green olives
2 tablespoons chopped mint
couscous, to serve

Serves 4

Preheat the oven to 375°F. Heat the stock and saffron together in a pan for 10 minutes to infuse.

Season the chicken thighs with black pepper, then dust liberally with the flour. Heat the oil in a heavy-bottomed casserole dish on the stove, add the chicken pieces and cook until lightly golden all over. Remove and set aside.

Add the diced squash, onions, lemon slices and garlic to the casserole and lightly cook until golden. Add the saffron stock and stir well to form a light sauce around the vegetables.

Return the chicken pieces to the sauce, add the honey and olives, cover with a lid and place in the oven to cook for 15–20 minutes until the chicken is cooked through. Stir the mint into the sauce, and serve with couscous.

4 PORTIONS: 434 CALS, 58G PROTEIN, 14G FAT, 3.6G SATURATED FAT, 20G CARBOHYDRATE, 12.1G SUGAR, 4.1G FIBER, 467MG SODIUM

burmese chicken

In this Burmese recipe the chicken is marinated in yogurt and spices, similar to an Indian tandoori. The yogurt makes the dish wonderfully succulent and tender.

4 x 6-ounce skinless chicken breasts
⅓ cup low-fat plain yogurt
1 tablespoon reduced salt soy sauce
½ teaspoon ground turmeric
1 tablespoon ground cumin
1 tablespoon ground cardamom
1 teaspoon chile powder
1-inch piece ginger, peeled and chopped
1 tablespoon sunflower oil
1 garlic clove, crushed
lime wedges, to garnish

For the tomato and ginger sauce
1 tablespoon sunflower oil
4 medium ripe firm plum tomatoes, chopped
1-inch piece ginger, peeled and chopped
1 small green chile, chopped
1 garlic clove, crushed
2 tablespoons roughly chopped fresh cilantro
½ cup tomato juice
juice of ½ lime
freshly ground black pepper

Serves 4

Place the chicken breasts in a dish. Combine the yogurt, soy sauce, turmeric, cumin, cardamom, chili and ginger in a small bowl and mix thoroughly together. Whisk in the oil and garlic, then pour over the chicken breasts. Mix well to ensure the chicken is well coated with the marinade. Place in the fridge for at least 6 hours, preferably overnight.

Preheat the oven to 350°F.

For the sauce, heat the oil in a non-stick saucepan, add the tomatoes, ginger, chili, garlic and cilantro and sweat for 8–10 minutes until vegetables have softened. Add the tomato juice, cook for another 10 minutes, then strain through a sieve into a clean pot. Season with black pepper, stir in the lime juice and keep warm.

Place the chicken breasts in a baking pan and bake for about 25 minutes until tender and cooked through.

Arrange the cooked chicken on serving plates, garnish with the lime wedges and serve with the sauce. Brown or wild rice makes a nice, simple accompaniment.

4 PORTIONS: 308 CALS, 45.9G PROTEIN, 9G FAT, 1.6G SATURATED FAT, 11.1G CARBOHYDRATE, 6.2G SUGAR, 1.2G FIBER, 394MG SODIUM

chicken with fennel, prunes and balsamic honey

For me there are few vegetables that taste equally as delicious raw and cooked. Fennel when raw is crisp, assertively aromatic and fresh. When cooked, its texture and taste are transformed into something altogether different, almost more bold and delicate.

4 x 6-ounce skinless chicken breasts
freshly ground black pepper
2 tablespoons sunflower oil
4 small-medium fennel, trimmed and cut into wedges
9 ounces frozen (or vacuum-packed) chestnuts
1 small bay leaf
3 teaspoons balsamic vinegar
2 tablespoons honey
⅔ cup chicken stock (see page 156; if using packaged products or bouillon cubes use "low-salt" varieties)
8 ounces ready-to-eat prunes

Serves 4

Season the chicken breasts with black pepper. Heat the oil in a non-stick pan, add the chicken breasts and cook until golden on both sides. Remove from the pan.

Add the fennel, chestnuts and bay leaf to the pan and cook for 5 minutes until lightly golden, turning the fennel often. Pour in the balsamic vinegar and honey to coat the fennel and chestnuts. Cook for another 4–5 minutes to infuse the flavors.

Add the stock, prunes and chicken, cover and cook over low heat for 10–12 minutes until the chicken is cooked through and the braising liquid forms a light sauce. Remove the bay leaf and adjust the seasoning before serving.

4 PORTIONS: 463 CALS, 46G PROTEIN, 10G FAT, 1.7G SATURATED FAT, 51G CARBOHYDRATE, 31.9.1G SUGAR, 8.8G FIBER, 143MG SODIUM

chicken with pineapple, ginger and lime

The combination of chicken and pineapple is nothing new; it is prepared throughout Asia and the Caribbean extensively. This is my variation of a dish I had in the Caribbean while working on the French island of St Martin. I prefer to use chicken legs separated into thigh and drumstick, but you could use breast of course.

4 large chicken thighs, skin removed
4 large chicken drumsticks, skin removed
freshly ground black pepper
pinch of cinnamon
pinch of turmeric
½ teaspon mild curry powder
½ teaspoon red chili flakes
2 tablespoons sunflower oil
4 scallions, finely chopped
juice of 2 limes

10 ounces fresh pineapple, cut into cubes (prepared weight)
1½-inch piece ginger
1 cup pineapple juice (no added sugar)
1 cup chicken stock (see page 156; if using packaged products or bouillon cubes use "low-salt" varieties)
4 medium tomatoes, blanched, deseeded and chopped

Serves 4

Preheat the oven to 350°F.

Place the chicken pieces in a dish, season with the black pepper, cinnamon, tumeric, curry powder and chili flakes, cover with plastic wrap and marinate overnight in the fridge.

Heat the oil in a large ovenproof casserole dish, add the chicken pieces and cook until brown all over. Drain the excess oil, add the remaining ingredients, bring to a boil, cover and place in the oven for up to 40 minutes or until the chicken is tender and the sauce reduced and slightly thickened. Serve immediately with brown rice.

4 PORTIONS: 330 CALS, 39G PROTEIN, 11G FAT, 2.6G SATURATED FAT, 20G CARBOHYDRATE, 18.7G SUGAR, 2G FIBER, 191MG SODIUM

rabbit cacciatore

"Cacciatore" in Italian means "hunter's style", and this dish, popular throughout Italy, is traditionally made with chicken. Rabbit makes a great alternative and again is one of those underestimated meats that seems to be making a little comeback, especially in the restaurant world. Also in this recipe I use porcini instead of button mushrooms, which adds another dimension to the dish. If unavailable use any type of common mushrooms. I recommend you serve this dish with creamy polenta in true Italian style.

4 large rabbit legs (or 8 large thighs)
freshly ground black pepper
pinch of dried oregano
1 tablespoon whole grain flour
2 tablespoons olive oil
1 garlic clove, crushed
1 onion, chopped
2 red peppers, deseeded and cut into 1-inch cubes
11 ounces porcini mushrooms
⅓ cup dry white wine

7 ounces canned, diced tomatoes (no added salt)
1 tablespoon tomato paste (no added salt)
2 teaspoons superfine sugar
1½ cups chicken stock (see page 156; if using packaged stock or cubes use "low salt" varieties)
10 fresh basil leaves

Serves 4

Season the rabbit with black pepper, rub all over with the dried oregano, then sprinkle the flour on top.

Heat the olive oil in a large heavy-bottomed pan, add the rabbit legs and cook until golden. Remove and set aside.

Add the garlic, onion, peppers and mushrooms to the pan and cook in the oil remaining in the pan. Add the white wine and boil for 2–3 minutes before adding the tomatoes, tomato paste, sugar and stock. Return to a boil.

Transfer the rabbit legs back to the sauce, cover and simmer for 40–45 minutes until the rabbit is tender. Stir the basil leaves into the sauce and cook for another 2 minutes. Adjust seasoning and serve on a bed of creamy polenta.

4 PORTIONS: 390 CALS, 42G PROTEIN, 16G FAT, 4.8G SATURATED FAT, 19G CARBOHYDRATE, 14.9G SUGAR, 2.8G FIBER, 156MG SODIUM

duck with cinnamon cherries and braised celery

Duck with cherries is a classic of French cuisine. By removing the duck's skin you remove a lot of the fat—the breast itself is quite lean.

1 tablespoon sunflower oil
4 x 6-ounce boneless and skinless
  duck breasts
9 ounces fresh or frozen cherries,
  pits removed
2 teaspoons reduced-sugar
  redcurrant jelly
⅓ cup red wine
pinch of ground cinnamon
3½ tablespoons Madeira
3½ tablespoons chicken stock (see
  page 156; if using packaged
  products or bouillon cubes use
  "low-salt" varieties)

For the celery
½ cup chicken stock (see
  page 156; if using packaged
  products or bouillon cubes use
  "low-salt" varieties)
few springs of thyme
8 celery stalks, peeled
  and cut on the bias into
  2-inch lengths
freshly ground black pepper

Serves 4

To braise the celery, bring the chicken stock and thyme to a boil, cook for 5 minutes, then lower the heat, add the celery and lightly braise under a lid for 5 minutes until the celery is just cooked and the stock almost evaporated. Season and keep warm.

Heat the oil in a non-stick pan, add the duck breasts and cook for 4–5 minutes on each side over medium heat until golden, a little longer if you don't want your duck pink. Remove from the pan and keep warm on a plate under foil.

Using the pan used for cooking the duck, add the cherries and redcurrant jelly and cook for 1 minute. Pour in the red wine, cinnamon, Madeira and chicken stock and simmer gently for 5–6 minutes until the sauce has reduced by half. Season with black pepper.

Thickly slice the duck and place on serving plates. Pour the cherry sauce over the duck and serve with the braised celery.

4 PORTIONS: 345 CALS, 36G PROTEIN, 14G FAT, 3.4G SATURATED FAT, 10G CARBOHYDRATE, 10.1G SUGAR, 1.7G FIBER, 265MG SODIUM

guinea hen with green peppercorn sauce and gingered carrots

Guinea hen, which tastes like slightly gamey chicken, makes a great alternative to chicken. Green peppercorns are purchased preserved in brine— simply rinse them under cold water before use to wash away some of the salt. Some tender, steamed broccoli would also go beautifully with the dish.

14 ounces young carrots, peeled and cut
  in half lengthways if big
1 tablespoon honey
2-inch piece ginger, peeled and finely
  chopped or grated
1 tablespoon sunflower oil
4 x 6-ounce guinea hen breasts, skins removed
freshly ground black pepper
4 tablespoons dry white wine
2 teaspoons superfine sugar
½ cup pink grapefruit juice (preferably fresh)
1 cup chicken stock (see page 156;
  if using packaged products or bouillon
  cubes, use "low-salt" varieties)
1 tablespoon green peppercorns in brine,
  rinsed and drained

Serves 4

Place the carrots in a pan, just cover with water, add the honey and ginger and bring to a boil. Reduce the heat and simmer until the carrots are just cooked and almost all the liquid has gone, leaving them in a gingery syrupy glaze. Keep warm.

Heat a non-stick pan and when hot add the oil. Season the guinea hen breasts with black pepper, add to the pan and cook for 3–4 minutes on each side until golden and cooked through. Remove and keep warm, covered with foil.

Return the pan to the heat, add the wine and sugar and cook together for 2 minutes. Add the grapefruit juice and stock and boil for 5 minutes until the sauce is reduced by one-third in volume.

Strain through a fine sieve, add the green peppercorns and season to taste.

To serve, arrange the cooked carrots on serving plates, top each with a cooked guinea hen breast and spoon the sauce on top. Serve with steamed new potatoes, if desired.

4 PORTIONS: 354 CALS, 40G PROTEIN, 9G FAT, 1.8G SATURATED FAT, 27G CARBOHYDRATE, 18.3G SUGAR, 2.5G FIBER, 293MG SODIUM

grilled duck breast with herb vinaigrette

Serving vinaigrettes as sauces for hot dishes is becoming increasingly popular. It is light and often more flavorsome than a contrived sauce, simple to put together and healthy as it's lower in fat.

1 teaspoon black peppercorns
1 teaspoon green peppercorns
 in brine, rinsed and drained
1 teaspoon pink peppercorns
 in brine, rinsed and drained
4 x 6-ounce skinless duck breasts
⅓ cup chicken stock
 (see page 156; if using
 packaged products or bouillon
 cubes use "low-salt" varieties)
2 small shallots, finely chopped
1 teaspoon thyme leaves

1 tablespoon chopped fresh
 tarragon
1 tablespoon chopped fresh
 flat-leaf parsley
1 tablespoon balsamic vinegar
4 tablespoons olive oil
2 garlic cloves, crushed
8 ounces wild mushrooms (or
 other mushrooms), cleaned
3½ ounces sundried tomatoes
 in oil, drained and dried
3½ ounces cooked peas
 freshly ground black pepper

Serves 4

Place the peppercorns in a mortar (or spice grinder) and pound to a coarse paste. Rub this paste liberally all over the duck breasts and leave to marinate for 30 minutes.

Heat the stock with the shallot, herbs and vinegar. Whisk in 2 tablespoons of the olive oil, bring to a boil, then remove from the heat and keep warm.

Heat a grill or grill pan. Brush the duck all over with 1 tablespoon of the oil and cook for 4–5 minutes on each side for medium, longer if you prefer your duck more well done. Transfer the duck to a plate, cover with foil and keep warm to allow the duck to rest.

Meanwhile, heat the remaining oil in a non-stick pan, add the garlic and mushrooms and cook for 2–3 minutes. Add the tomatoes and peas and cook for another 2–3 minutes. Season with black pepper. Arrange the vegetables on 4 serving plates, top each with a duck breast and spoon the warm vinaigrette on top. Serve with sautéed potatoes.

4 PORTIONS: 352 CALS, 43G PROTEIN, 15G FAT, 2.5G SATURATED FAT, 11G CARBOHYDRATE, 4.7G SUGAR, 3G FIBER, 354MG SODIUM

guinea hen with apple, wild mushrooms and tarragon

I made this recipe using chicken for dinner while visiting friends in the beautiful Vosges countryside of France. It turned out well made with the ingredients we had to hand in their kitchen and with those purchased at the wonderful local market in Gérardmer. There are excellent wild mushroom varieties in the market, especially in autumn, and certain ones are available year-round.

1 tablespoon sunflower oil
4 x 6-ounce skinless boneless
 guinea hen breasts
freshly ground black pepper
7 ounces mixed wild mushrooms
 (or button mushrooms),
 cleaned and sliced
½ garlic clove, crushed
⅓ cup apple juice (no added
 sugar)

½ cup chicken stock (see page 156;
 if using packaged products or
 bouillon cubes use "low-salt"
 varieties)
⅓ cup 1% milk
1 tablespoon cornstarch
1 teaspoon Dijon mustard
2 tablespoons chopped
 fresh tarragon

Serves 4

Heat a heavy-bottomed pan with a shot of oil-water spray (see page 36). Season the guinea hen breasts with black pepper, add to the pan and sear quickly on both sides, without allowing to brown. Add the wild mushrooms and garlic and cook for another 2–3 minutes.

Remove the guinea hen and set aside. Add the apple juice and stock and cook for 2–3 minutes.

Whisk the milk and cornstarch together and then whisk both into the stock. Simmer for 5 minutes. Add the mustard and tarragon, then return the guinea hen to the sauce. Cook for another 5-6 minutes until the hen is tender and the sauce is thick enough to coat. Season with black pepper and serve.

4 PORTIONS: 244 CALS, 39G PROTEIN, 5G FAT, 1.8G SATURATED FAT, 7G CARBOHYDRATE, 3.8G SUGAR, 0.4G FIBER, 193MG SODIUM

pheasant scallops with endive and cranberries

Pheasants are available from October to February when the game season is really under way. You can generally purchase either the whole bird or just the boneless breasts. Game birds are very underrated. I believe due to the fact that people are unsure how to cook them. In this recipe the pheasant breasts only are used, pound out into thin scallops, making the cooking and timing much easier and reliable. Almond polenta makes a wonderful accompaniment but do check the label of instant polenta as some brands contain added salt.

4 x 6-ounce pheasant breasts, boneless, skin removed
4 Belgain endive, leaves separated, shredded
   coarsely
1 tablespoon maple syrup
2 tablespoons sunflower oil
1 tablespoon cider vinegar
½ cup cranberry juice
1 tablespoon cranberry jelly (reduced-sugar if available)
½ cup chicken stock (see page 156; if using
   packaged products or bouillon cubes use
   "low-salt" varieties)
4½ ounces frozen cranberries
freshly ground black pepper

For the almond polenta
2 cups 1% milk
1 small garlic clove, crushed
few thyme sprigs
4 ounces instant polenta
2 ounces ground almondsv

Serves 4

Place each pheasant breast between 2 sheets of plastic wrap and, using a kitchen mallet or rolling pin, lightly pound them out to 1-inch thick scallops.

For the polenta, bring the milk, garlic and thyme to a boil, heat for 5 minutes, then remove the thyme. Slowly sprinkle in the polenta and ground almonds, stirring constantly. Reduce the heat to the lowest setting, simmer the polenta for 8–10 minutes or until the polenta is cooked and the consistency of wet mashed potatoes. Keep warm.

Heat a non-stick pan, add the endive, maple syrup and $1^2/_3$ cups of water and cook over medium heat until the endive is softened and caramelized. Remove from the heat and keep warm.

Heat the oil in a large non-stick pan, add the scallops of pheasant and cook over high heat for 2–3 minutes on each side until pink and tender. Transfer to a plate, cover with foil and keep warm.

Add the vinegar, cranberry juice, cranberry jelly and stock to the pan and cook for 2–3 minutes. Strain through a fine sieve back into the pan. Add the cranberries and cook for 4–5 minutes or until softened. Season with black pepper.

Place the polenta onto serving plates, top with a pheasant scallop and the caramelized endive. Reheat the cranberry sauce for 2 minutes, then pour over the top of each plate and serve.

4 PORTIONS: 556 CALS, 47.8G PROTEIN, 21.1G FAT, 4.6G SATURATED FAT, 44.2G CARBOHYDRATE, 19.8G SUGAR, 3.1G FIBER, 136MG SODIUM

turkey paillard with lentils and apricot vinaigrette

Turkey doesn't always have to be roasted you know! Here the breast is pounded into scallops, or paillards to use the more old-fashioned term, then grilled until succulent. Serve with earthy chestnuts and Puy lentils and a sweet apricot sauce. Steamed broccoli or spinach make a nice accompaniment.

2 tablespoons sunflower oil
1 onion, peeled and
 finely chopped
12 ounces Puy lentils
9 ounces cooked frozen
 chestnuts (or vacuum packed)
4 x 6-ounce scallops of
 turkey breast

Serves 4

For the vinaigrette
8 dried apricots, soaked in hot
 water until plump, drained,
 dried and chopped
1 tablespoon balsamic vinegar
½ teaspoon Dijon mustard
4 tablespoons olive oil
1 teaspoon chopped fresh
 rosemary
1 tablespoon honey
freshly ground black pepper

Heat the oil in a heavy-bottomed pan, add the onion and cook until golden. Add the lentils and enough water to cover, then cook for 15–20 minutes or until just tender, but still retaining a bite. Drain well and keep warm. Toss in the chestnuts.

Make the vinaigrette by mixing all the ingredients in a bowl. Season to taste with black pepper.

Preheat a grill or grill pan. When hot, season the turkey with black pepper and cook on the grill for 3–4 minutes each side until cooked through.

Add a little of the vinaigrette to the lentils, and spoon onto individual serving plates. Top each with a grilled turkey paillard, spoon the remaining apricot vinaigrette on top and serve.

4 PORTIONS: 786 CALS, 72.7G PROTEIN, 21.7G FAT, 3.2G SATURATED FAT, 79.9G CARBOHYDRATE, 19G SUGAR, 12.2G FIBER, 149MG SODIUM

zaatar-spiced chicken with arabic slaw

Zaatar is a Middle Eastern spice mix consisting of dried thyme, sesame seeds and sumac, a lemon-flavored berry, which can be found in good gourmet and specialty markets. Zaatar can also be purchased ready-blended from Middle Eastern stores. Panko breadcrumbs are a dry and crispy breadcrumb used extensively in Japanese cooking. They add a wonderful crunch to fried foods and are well worth finding. Serve with some toasted whole grain pita bread wedges.

1 tablespoon dried thyme
1 tablespoon sesame seeds
1 tablespoon sumac
3½ ounces panko breadcrumbs
freshly ground black pepper
1½ pounds chicken thighs, skinless
 and boneless, cut into 1-inch cubes
2 eggs, beaten with 1 tablespoon
 water
1 tablespoon olive oil

Serves 4

For the slaw
1 red onion, peeled and
 thinly sliced
½ small cucumber,
 thinly sliced
1 red pepper, deseeded and
 thinly sliced
2 ounces fresh mint leaves
2 ounces fresh cilantro leaves
juice of ½ lemon
2 tablespoons reduced-fat
 mayonnaise

In a dish, prepare the zaatar by mixing together the thyme, sesame seeds and sumac. Add the panko crumbs and a little black pepper.

Dip the chicken pieces in the beaten egg mixture until covered, then into the spice mix. Thread onto 4 metal or pre-soaked wooden skewers, 5–6 pieces per skewer.

Heat the olive oil in a large non-stick pan, add the skewers and cook over medium heat for 8–10 minutes, turning often. Meanwhile, toss all the ingredients for the slaw in a bowl and season with a little black pepper.

Serve the skewers with a pile of the slaw alongside, and with hot toasted pita wedges.

4 PORTIONS: 416 CALS, 43G PROTEIN, 17G FAT, 4G SATURATED FAT, 24G CARBOHYDRATE, 4.6G SUGAR, 1.6G FIBER, 344MG SODIUM

spanish-style lamb stew

In Spain this typical lamb stew is known as "Caldereta"; this is my adaption of the dish.

4 garlic cloves, crushed
2 bay leaves
1 teaspoon Spanish smoked paprika
freshly ground black pepper
1 cup tomato paste (no added salt)
1 teaspoon superfine sugar
2 tablespoons red wine vinegar
6 x 6-ounce lamb fillets, trimmed of all visible fat

1 tablespoon olive oil
2 onions, finely chopped
2 green peppers, deseeded and cut into large pieces
1 head fennel, cut into large pieces
14 ounces baby new potatoes
2 tablespoons chopped fresh flat-leaf parsley
1 tablespoon chopped fresh oregano

Serves 6

In a blender, place the garlic, bay leaves, smoked paprika, black pepper, tomato paste, sugar and vinegar with a little water and process into a marinade paste.

Cut the lamb into large cubes, place in a dish then toss with the marinade. Cover with plastic wrap and leave to marinate for 2 hours at room temperature.

Heat the olive oil in a heavy-bottomed non-stick pan, add the onion, peppers and fennel and cook for 4–5 minutes until the vegetables are slightly softened. Add the marinated meat and juices to the pan, cover with water, bring to a boil, reduce the heat and simmer.

After 30 minutes, add the new potatoes, parsley and oregano and simmer in the sauce for another 30 minutes or until cooked. Adjust the seasoning and serve.

4 PORTIONS: 437 CALS, 34.1G PROTEIN, 23.4G FAT, 10.7G SATURATED FAT, 23.8G CARBOHYDRATE, 12.1G SUGAR, 4.1G FIBER, 116MG SODIUM

rump of lamb niçoise with aioli

A dish reminiscent of the colors and flavors of Provence.

1 eggplant, cut into large cubes
1 green zucchini, thickly sliced
1 yellow zucchini, thickly sliced
1 head fennel, cut into large cubes
1 red pepper, deseeded and cut into thick strips
1 yellow pepper, deseeded and cut into thick strips
8 garlic cloves, peeled
1 tablespoon roughly chopped fresh rosemary
2 tablespoons olive oil
freshly ground black pepper
4 x 6-ounce lamb rumps, all excess fat removed

For the aioli
⅓ cup reduced-fat mayonnaise
½ garlic clove, crushed
juice of ¼ lemon

Serves 4

Preheat the oven to 400°F.

Toss the vegetables and rosemary in the olive oil, season with black pepper, place in a roasting pan and roast for 30–40 minutes until tender and lightly charred. Season the lamb with black pepper. After 20 minutes, place the lamb rumps on the vegetables and continue to roast until all ingredients are cooked.

For the aioli, mix all the ingredients together in a bowl and season with black pepper.

Divide the vegetables between 4 serving plates, carve each lamb rump into 4 slices and place on top of the vegetables. Drizzle the aioli around the plate and serve.

4 PORTIONS: 410 CALS, 34.4G PROTEIN, 25.5G FAT, 7.9G SATURATED FAT, 11.6G CARBOHYDRATE, 8.7G SUGAR, 4.6G FIBER, 350MG SODIUM

lamb osso bucco (indian style)

You may be confused by this dish. Classic Osso Bucco is traditionally an Italian dish made with veal shank, which is fairly expensive and often difficult to obtain. In this recipe I use leg of lamb, and flavor the sauce with wonderful Indian spices using the same method. A dish for hearty meat eaters, serve with saffron rice.

2 garlic cloves, crushed
4-inch piece ginger, peeled and chopped
⅓ cup low-fat plain yogurt
4 x 9–10-ounce lean leg of lamb steaks
freshly ground black pepper
2 tablespoons sunflower oil
1 onion, peeled and chopped
1 red chile, finely chopped
1 teaspoon curry powder
½ teaspoon ground turmeric
1 teaspoon ground cumin
1 teaspoon ground cardamom
14½-ounce can diced tomatoes
1 tablespoon tomato paste
1 tablespoon brown sugar
1 quart chicken stock (see page 156; if using
   packaged stock or cubes use "low salt" varieties)
1 tablespoon chopped fresh mint
1 tablespoon chopped fresh cilantro

Serves 4

First place the garlic and ginger in a blender with the yogurt and process into a paste. Place the lamb steaks in a dish, season with black pepper then add the yogurt mixture, combine well, cover with plastic wrap and place in the fridge to marinate overnight.

Preheat the oven to 350°F.

Heat the oil in a heavy-bottomed ovenproof casserole dish. When hot, remove the lamb from its marinade, wiping off any excess, then add to the pan and cook until golden on both sides. Remove from the pan and set aside. Reserve the marinade.

Add the onion and chili to the pan and cook gently until onions are lightly golden. Add the curry powder, turmeric, cumin and cardamom and cook for 1 minute. Add the marinade, tomatoes, tomato paste, sugar and stock and bring to a boil.

Return the lamb to the sauce, cover the casserole with a lid and place in the oven to braise for up to 1 hour until the lamb is tender. Adjust the seasoning of the sauce. Add the mint and cilantro to garnish.

Place each lamb steak on a bed of saffron rice, then pour the braising sauce on top and serve.

4 PORTIONS: 470 CALS, 50.3G PROTEIN, 24.5G FAT, 9.7G SATURATED FAT, 13G CARBOHYDRATE, 9.5G SUGAR, 1.8G FIBER, 270MG SODIUM

mustard lamb with garlic and mint

To roast the garlic, simply break into cloves, place them in a pouch of foil with a spoonful of olive oil and bake at 350°F for up to 30 minutes until the garlic is soft and lightly caramelized. Leave to cool, then slip the cooked garlic cloves from their skins.

4 tablespoons olive oil
8 lamb cutlets, trimmed of excess fat
freshly ground black pepper
3½ tablespoons dry white wine
1 cup chicken stock (see page 156; if using packaged-products or bouillon cubes use "low-salt" varieties)
1 teaspoon Dijon mustard
1 tablespoon mint jelly
4 zucchini, cut into thick slices

For the garlic oil
3 tablespoons olive oil
12 roasted garlic cloves (see introduction)
2 tomatoes, blanched, skinned, deseeded and cut into small dice
juice of ½ lemon
1 tablespoon chopped fresh mint

Serves 4

Heat 2 tablespoons of the olive oil in a non-stick pan, season the lamb with black pepper and cook for 3–4 minutes on each side until pink (longer if you prefer them more well done). Remove from the pan and keep warm.

Add the wine and stock to the pan and boil for 5 minutes. Add the mustard and mint jelly and stir together to form a sauce.

In a separate pan, sauté the zucchini in the remaining oil for 4–5 minutes until golden and tender. Season with black pepper, remove and keep warm.

For the garlic oil, heat the olive oil, add the roasted garlic, tomatoes, lemon juice and mint and cook over very low heat for 2–3 minutes to infuse. Season with black pepper.

To serve arrange the lamb on a bed of zucchini, pour a little of the mustard mint sauce around the plate, and a little roasted garlic oil over the lamb.

4 PORTIONS: 456 CALS, 30.5G PROTEIN, 32.6G FAT, 9G SATURATED FAT, 9.7G CARBOHYDRATE, 7.3G SUGAR, 2.3G FIBER, 135MG SODIUM

pork chop with mixed summer beans and grilled peach

This is a lovely dish to make during the summer when peaches are available, and out of this world. Saying that, there are some good quality preserved or frozen varieties on the market, which could be substituted. For the best results peel the peaches.

1 tablespoon sunflower oil
4 x 6-ounce pork chops, all excess fat removed
freshly ground black pepper
1 tablespoon reduced-sugar peach jam
2 tablespoons balsamic vinegar
2 large peaches, halved and pitted,

⅓ cup dry sherry
⅓ cup peach nectar
⅔ cup chicken stock (see page 156; if using packaged products or bouillon cubes use "low-salt" varieties)
9 ounces yellow wax beans
10½ ounces green beans, trimmed

Serves 4

Heat a non-stick pan and add the oil. Season the pork chops with black pepper, add to the pan and cook over medium heat for 4–5 minutes on each side until golden. Remove from the pan and keep warm.

Return the pan to the heat, add the peach jam and vinegar and cook for 30 seconds. Add the peach halves, cut-side down and lightly caramelize in the vinegar syrup. When slightly softened, remove and keep warm.

To the pan add the sherry, peach nectar and stock, reduce by half in volume, then strain through a sieve into a clean pan.

Cook the beans in separate pans of boiling water until tender, then drain and season with black pepper.

Arrange the beans on 4 individual serving plates and top each with a cooked pork chop. Place a caramelized peach on each chop, spoon the sauce over each plate and serve.

4 PORTIONS: 333 CALS, 43G PROTEIN, 10G FAT, 2.2G SATURATED FAT, 16G CARBOHYDRATE, 14.6G SUGAR, 4.4G FIBER, 123MG SODIUM

lamb neck fillet with red cabbage caponata

A caponata is a sweet and sour relish, served as an accompaniment to fish or meat dishes. Traditionally made with eggplant and celery, this one to serve with the lamb is made with red cabbage following the same principles. Serve with cubes of roasted potatoes cooked with garlic and sage.

4 x 6-ounce lamb neck fillets
2 tablespoons olive oil
freshly ground black pepper
1 tablespoon fresh thyme leaves
1⅓ cups chicken stock

For the caponata
2 tablespoons sunflower oil

1 small red cabbage, very
   thinly sliced
1 red onion, thinly sliced
½ cup red wine vinegar
4 tablespoons maple syrup
2 ounces raisins, soaked in
   water for 30 minutes, drained
   and dried
2 tablespoons toasted pine nuts

Serves 4

Preheat the oven to 400°F.

For the caponata, heat the oil in a heavy-bottomed pan, add the red cabbage and red onion, reduce the heat and cook, stirring occasionally, for about 20 minutes until the cabbage and onion have softened.

Add the vinegar and maple syrup and continue cooking until the vegetables are cooked and caramelized. Add the raisins and pine nuts and mix well. Remove from the heat and keep warm. Brush the lamb fillets all over with the olive oil and season with black pepper and thyme.

Heat a non-stick, ovenproof pan. When hot, add the lamb and sear, turning occasionally, until golden all over. Place in the oven and cook for 10–12 minutes. Remove and keep warm. Add the stock to the pan juices, return to a boil on the stove and season with black pepper.

Cut the lamb into thick slices, arrange on top of the cabbage, pour pan juices over the lamb and serve.

4 PORTIONS: 549 CALS, 32.7G PROTEIN, 35.8G FAT, 12.3G SATURATED FAT, 25.5G CARBOHYDRATE, 22.9G SUGAR, 3.2G FIBER, 138MG SODIUM

pork chop with chard, raisins and green sauce

It is vitally important not to overcook pork. I prefer to serve it when it is still a little pink but this is not advisable for pregnant women, young children or the elderly. However, adding a little water during the cooking process should help keep it moist and juicy.

2 tablespoons olive oil
1 garlic clove, crushed
8 large fresh Swiss chard leaves, roughly chopped
2 ounces raisins, soaked in warm water, for 30 minutes, drained
2 ounces dried apricots, cut into pieces
4 x 6-ounce pork chops, fat removed
freshly ground black pepper

For the green sauce
2 tablespoons chopped fresh flat-leaf parsley
2 tablespoons chopped fresh mint
½ teaspoon Dijon mustard
1 tablespoon capers, rinsed, drained and chopped
1 garlic clove, crushed
½ teaspoon sugar
3 tablespoons olive oil
1 tablespoon white wine vinegar

Serves 4

Quickly prepare the green sauce. Place the herbs, mustard, capers, garlic and sugar in a small blender, add the oil and vinegar and process into a coarse paste.

In a pan, heat half the olive oil and garlic together. Add the chard stems and season with a little pepper. Add ⅓ cup water and cook for 5 minutes. Add the chard leaves, apricots and raisins and cook for another 3–4 minutes until tender.

Meanwhile, heat a non-stick pan and add the remaining oil. Season the pork chops with the pepper, add to the pan and brown on both sides. Reduce the heat, add a spoonful of water, cover the pan and cook gently for 5–6 minutes until just cooked. Keep warm.

To serve, place the pork chops on serving plates, garnish with a spoonful of the green sauce and place the braised chard alongside. Serve immediately.

4 PORTIONS: 381 CALS, 36.2G PROTEIN, 19.3G FAT, 3.6G SATURATED FAT, 16.8G CARBOHYDRATE, 14.5G SUGAR, 1.3G FIBER, 356MG SODIUM

pork schnitzel with apple, sage, celery root remoulade

Schnitzel is the term for a German or Austrian meat preparation consisting of a pounded out thin scallop of veal or pork in a crispy crumb crust. I like to serve it with mashed potatoes or small roasted new potatoes.

4 x 6-ounce pork chops or loin, any bone and
    visible fat removed
1 egg, beaten
3 tablespoons 1% milk
3 ounces dried whole grain breadcrumbs
3 tablespoons sunflower oil
2 Granny Smith apples, cored and cut
    into 6 wedges
1 teaspoon brown sugar
¾ cup apple juice (no added sugar)
⅓ cup chicken stock (see page 156;
    if using packaged stock or bouillon cubes use
    "low salt" varieties)
8 small sage leaves

For the remoulade
1 medium celery root (approx 11 ounces), peeled
juice of ½ lemon
2 teaspoons Dijon mustard
2 tablespoons reduced-fat mayonnaise
freshly ground black pepper

Serves 4

Using a kitchen mallet or large rolling pin, lightly flatten the pork chops between 2 sheets of plastic wrap. Mix the egg and milk together in a bowl. Dip the scallops of pork in the egg mix then dredge them through the breadcrumbs, ensuring they are well coated.

To make the remoulade, grate the celery root coarsely in a bowl, then add the lemon juice. Leave for 5 minutes, then squeeze out all the excess liquid in your hands. Dry in a cloth, then place in a bowl. Stir in the mustard and mayonnaise and season with black pepper.

Heat a non-stick pan with 1 tablespoon of the oil, add the apple wedges and cook for 1 minute until golden.

Sprinkle in the sugar and lightly caramelize in the pan. Add the apple juice, stock and sage and cook until the apples are tender and the sauce reduced by half in volume.

Heat another large non-stick pan with the remaining 2 tablespoons of oil, when hot add the schnitzel, cook for 2–3 minutes until golden and crispy.

Spoon the apples with the sauce onto serving plates, top each with a schnitzel, garnish with the celery root remoulade and serve.

4 PORTIONS: 460 CALS, 44G PROTEIN, 20.6G FAT, 4.4G SATURATED FAT, 26.1G CARBOHYDRATE, 16.4G SUGAR, 4.8G FIBER, 415MG SODIUM

beef fillet with sweet potato and hazelnut purée

This dish is an adaptation of a recipe by my good friend Dean Fearing, a pioneer of Southern cuisine in Texas during the nineties. Nutella is a popular chocolate and hazelnut spread, available in most supermarkets.

½ tablespoon maple syrup
1 tablespoon balsamic vinegar
1 teaspoon coarsely ground black pepper
½ teaspoon fresh thyme leaves
4 x 5-ounce beef fillet steaks
2 large sweet potatoes
2 tablespoons margarine spread
1 tablespoon Nutella (chocolate and hazelnut spread)
freshly ground black pepper
2 tablespoons sunflower oil
10½ ounces baby onions
1 teaspoon superfine sugar
1⅓ cups chicken stock (see page 156;
    if using packaged products or bouillon cubes
    use "low-salt" varieties)
7 ounces mixed wild mushrooms, cleaned and trimmed

Serves 4

In a shallow dish, combine the maple syrup with the balsamic vinegar, black pepper and thyme. Add the beef fillets, combine well with the marinade, cover and leave in the fridge to marinate overnight.

Preheat the oven to 350°F.

Prick the sweet potatoes all over with a small fork, place them on a sheet of foil, scrunch it up to seal up the foil, place on a baking sheet in the oven for 30 minutes or until soft. Leave to cool slightly before peeling.

Pass the sweet potatoes through a sieve or mash until smooth, add the spread and Nutella, mix again and season well with black pepper. Keep warm.

Heat 1 tablespoon of oil in a non-stick pan, add the baby onions and cook until golden. Add the sugar and continue to cook until caramelized. Add the stock and simmer until tender. Add the wild mushrooms, cook for 2 minutes, and set aside.

Heat the remaining oil in a non-stick pan and cook the beef fillets until golden all over—3–4 minutes on each side (for medium), longer if you prefer them more well done. Remove from the pan and keep warm. Add 2 tablespoons of the beef marinade to the pan, along with the reserved onion and mushroom mixture and heat gently.

Arrange the sweet potatoes on serving plates, top with beef, pour the sauce over the dish and serve.

4 PORTIONS: 479 CALS, 34.8G PROTEIN, 20.5G FAT, 5.4G SATURATED FAT, 41.4G CARBOHYDRATE, 16.2G SUGAR, 5G FIBER, 217MG SODIUM

spice-grilled venison with beet and apple risotto

Venison is a nice lean choice of game. The spice crust adds a fragrant heat and works well with the slightly sweet-tasting risotto. Farmed venison is good and widely available, although wild venison does have a more intense flavor. I often serve this dish with a purée of broccoli.

8 x 3-ounce lean venison medallions
½ teaspoon black peppercorns, lightly cracked
1 teaspoon fennel seeds, lightly cracked
2 tablespoons chopped fresh cilantro
1 tablespoon chopped fresh mint
1-inch piece ginger, peeled and grated
1 tablespoon olive oil

For the risotto
2⅓ cups chicken stock (see page 156; if using packaged products or bouillon cubes use "low-salt" varieties)
⅓ cup red wine
juice of 1 small raw beet
2 tablespoons olive oil
1 small onion, chopped
1 large cooked beet, cut into small dice
9 ounces risotto rice (e.g. Arborio)
½ Granny Smith apple, peeled and grated
2 tablespoons of unsalted butter, to finish

Serves 4

Place the venison medallions in a shallow dish. In a bowl, mix together all the seasoning ingredients except the oil. Liberally season the venison all over with the spice mix, cover with plastic wrap and leave to marinate at room temperature for 1 hour.

For the risotto, place the stock, wine and half the beet juice in a pan. Bring to a boil and simmer for 5 minutes.

Heat the oil in a heavy-bottomed saucepan, add the onion and beet and cook gently for 2 minutes. Add the rice and stir to combine well.

Add the hot stock gradually, about ½ cup at a time, ensuring it is completely evaporated before adding more, stirring constantly. This will take up to 20–25 minutes in all, by which time the rice should be just tender while retaining a little bite (al dente).

Add the grated apple along with the remaining beet juice and butter to finish, which will give it added richness. Season with a little black pepper.

While the risotto is cooking, cook your venison. Heat a grill or grill pan until hot, brush the venison medallions liberally with a little oil and cook on the hot grill for 3–4 minutes each side for pink or longer if you prefer your meat more well done.

Spoon the beet risotto onto serving plates, top with the spiced venison medallions and serve.

4 PORTIONS: 505 CALS, 42G PROTEIN, 13G FAT, 2.7G SATURATED FAT, 56G CARBOHYDRATE, 5.2G SUGAR, 2G FIBER, 145MG SODIUM

chapter five

desserts

almond milk custard with saffron and rosewater

Smooth, silky custards flavored with saffron and rosewater are inspired by the Middle East. Garnish with some juicy raspberries or wild strawberries for an extra treat.

4 tablespoons whole blanched almonds, toasted
3¼ cups 1% milk
2 tablespoons superfine sugar
½ teaspoon vanilla extract,
good pinch of saffron
2 eggs, plus 2 egg yolks

2 tablespoons custard powder
2 tablespoons rosewater
1 tablespoons Amaretto liquor (optional)
fresh berries and toasted, slivered almonds, to serve
confectioners' sugar, to dust

Serves 4

Place the whole almonds in a blender and process until finely ground. Bring the milk, half the sugar and the vanilla extract to a boil in a pan. Remove from the heat, add the ground almonds and saffron and leave to infuse for 15 minutes.

In a bowl, whisk together the eggs, egg yolks and remaining sugar until light and fluffy, then whisk in the custard powder. Whisk in the almond milk, rosewater and Amaretto, if using.

Clean the saucepan and return the custard to it. Heat gently, stirring constantly, until it thickens (do not allow to boil). Pour the custard into individual gratin-style dishes or ramekins. Place on a tray and transfer to the fridge for up to 2 hours or until firmly set.

To serve, top with the chosen berries and slivered almonds and dust liberally with confectioners' sugar.

4 PORTIONS: 260 CALS, 11G PROTEIN, 15G FAT, 3.3G SATURATED FAT, 20G CARBOHYDRATE, 15.5G SUGAR, 0.9G FIBER, 104MG SODIUM

bananas "en papillote" with banana sorbet

Opening these baked paper parcels at the table and releasing the aroma of the sweet fragrant spices adds a little theater to the dessert. Bananas are a good source of potassium, which can help lower blood pressure; apricots and orange juice also provide potassium.

1¾ cups fresh apricots, pitted and chopped
½ cup orange juice (fresh or packaged)
1 tablespoon superfine sugar
2 vanilla pods, split lengthways

4 small cinnamon sticks
8 star anise pods
4 medium ripe bananas
banana sorbet, to serve (see page 148)
few small mint leaves, to garnish

Serves 4

Preheat the oven to 400°F.

Place the apricots, orange juice and sugar in a pan, add the vanilla, cinnamon and star anise pods and cook gently for 10 minutes, until the apricots are very soft. Remove the spices and set aside.

Transfer the apricots to a blender and process until very smooth.

Cut 4 pieces of aluminium foil each 10 x 6 inches and lay on a work surface. Place one peeled banana on each piece and fold up the sides of the foil into a neat boat shape.

Pour the apricot sauce over the bananas and stick in the reserved spices (vanilla, anise pods and cinnamon). Fold up the edges of each parcel and seal it by scrunching it up at the top. Place on a baking sheet and bake for 15–20 minutes.

Serve the parcels to your guests at the table. Once opened, serve with banana sorbet and garnish with chopped mint.

4 PORTIONS: 156 CALS, 2G PROTEIN, 1G FAT, 0.1G SATURATED FAT, 38G CARBOHYDRATE, 34.9G SUGAR, 2.7G FIBER, 7MG SODIUM

fruit skewers in balsamic vinegar syrup

A simple and delicious dessert. You can vary the fruits according to the season and to your personal preference but remember the fruits chosen must be firm enough to withstand the grilling process and be not too ripe. The skewers can be prepared in advance, then just cooked in the syrup when needed, though fruit cut and left to stand ahead of time loses a lot of its vitamin C content. The wooden skewers should be soaked for 1 hour in water prior to use: this stops them becoming charred while grilling, especially when using on a hot charcoal grill.

2 nectarines
4 red plums
2 bananas
zest and juice of 1 orange
1 cup of pineapple, cut into bite-sized chunks
    (prepared weight)
12 large strawberries, halved
2 tablespoons Grand Marnier or other
    orange liqueur (optional)

For the syrup
2 tablespoons brown sugar
¼ cup balsamic vinegar

Serves 4

Cut the nectarines and plums in half, remove the pits, then cut each half into bite-sized chunks. Peel the bananas and cut into 1-inch thick slices.

Place the orange juice and zest and liqueur, if using, in a bowl, add all the fruit pieces and toss together. Leave for 30 minutes.

Thread the marinated fruit pieces onto prepared wooden sticks, alternating colors for added visual appeal, allowing 2 skewers per person. Refrigerate until needed.

To serve, preheat a grill over very high heat. Heat the sugar and vinegar together in a small saucepan for 3–4 minutes or until it becomes syrupy. Place the skewers on a grill pan, brush liberally with the syrup, then place under the grill to glaze for about 4–5 minutes, turning them regularly. Drizzle any excess syrup over the top and serve.

4 PORTIONS: 176 CALS, 2.6G PROTEIN, 0.4G FAT, 0.1G SATURATED FAT, 42.9G CARBOHYDRATE, 41.8G SUGAR, 3.4G FIBER, 10MG SODIUM

caramelized apricots with grapes and rosemary honey

For the purist who craves perfection, peeling the grapes with a small sharp knife lets them absorb the flavors of the juices in the pan. Whatever you decide it will be delicious! I have rarely used butter in this book, but here a little good, unsalted butter is essential.

12 fresh apricots, not too ripe (canned in juice is fine)
1¼ cups seedless white grapes, peeled (unpeeled are fine)
2 tablespoons honey
2 tablespoons of unsalted butter
1 tablespoon brandy
1 teaspoon rosemary leaves, coarsely chopped
juice of 1 lemon

2 tablespoons slivered almonds, lightly toasted, to serve
low-fat plain yogurt, to serve

Serves 4

Halve the apricots and remove the pits.

Heat a large non-stick pan, add the apricots and grapes, then the honey and the butter and quickly caramelize over high heat until golden.

Add the brandy and cook for 30 seconds, then add 4 tablespoons water. Add the rosemary and lemon juice and toss to form a sauce around the fruit.

Divide the fruit between 4 serving plates, scatter with the toasted almonds and serve with the yogurt.

4 PORTIONS: 130 CALS, 2G PROTEIN, 1G FAT, 0.7G SATURATED FAT, 28G CARBOHYDRATE, 27.7G SUGAR, 2.3G FIBER, 5MG SODIUM

fromage frais with gooseberries and elderflower

This is one of the simplest yet tastiest dishes I know. The fromage frais is lightened to the texture of silky snow and topped with a fragrant and delicious honey-flavored gooseberry compôte flavored with elderflower. Gooseberries, to my sadness, have a very short early summer season, so use them at any opportunity to make wonderful sauces, tarts, puddings and compôtes. This dish is also great served for breakfast.

2 gelatin leaves (or ½ tablespoon granulated gelatin)
zest of ½ lemon
1 cup low-fat fromage frais (or low-fat cream cheese)
1 tablespoon elderflower cordial
1 egg white
1 ounce superfine sugar

For the gooseberry compote
2 tablespoons elderflower cordial
¼ cup honey
½ pound gooseberries, not too ripe
1 teaspoon lemon juice

Serves 4

For the gooseberry compôte, place the elderflower cordial and honey in a pan, bring to a boil, then reduce the heat to a low simmer. Add the gooseberries and cook gently for 8–10 minutes, until the gooseberries are soft and the liquid is syrupy. Leave to cool and add lemon juice.

Place the gelatin leaves in a bowl, just cover with cold water and leave for 4–5 minutes to soften. Meanwhile, heat the elderflower cordial in a small pan. Squeeze out the gelatin and stir into the warmed cordial to melt, then leave to cool slightly.

Place the fromage frais and lemon zest in a bowl, pour in the cordial and gelatin liquid and mix well.

Whisk the egg white with half the sugar until stiff, then fold in the remaining sugar. Fold the whisked egg white gently into the fromage frais, ensuring it is well combined. Divide the mixture between 4 serving bowls or glasses and place in the fridge to set for up to 1 hour.

Top each fromage frais with some gooseberry compôte and serve.

4 PORTIONS: 165 CALS, 10G PROTEIN, 0G FAT, 0G SATURATED FAT, 33G CARBOHYDRATE, 32.6G SUGAR, 1.4G FIBER, 60MG SODIUM

citrus fruit float

This dessert takes me back to my childhood days, enjoying Mom's simple ice cream floats made by pouring Coca-Cola over creamy vanilla ice cream. In my more exotic version I combine a melange of colorful citrus fruits and an exotic lychee-based sorbet. You will find canned lychees work best for this sorbet and, of course, they are more readily available in stores.

For the sorbet
2 tablespoons superfine sugar
⅓ cup water
1 x 14½-ounce can lychees in syrup
⅓ cup pink grapefruit juice (preferably fresh with no added sugar)
2 tablespoons white rum (optional)

For the float
1 sweet orange
1 pink grapefruit
1 lime
1 piece preserved ginger, finely chopped, plus 4 tablespoons of syrup from the jar
2 lemongrass stalks, outer leaves removed, inner core finely chopped
1 cup cream soda

Serves 4

For the sorbet, place the sugar and water in a pan. Slowly bring to a boil, simmer for 5 minutes until the sugar has dissolved. Remove from the heat and leave to cool.

Drain the lychees, reserving ½ cup of their syrup. Purée the lychees in a blender, add the reserved lychee syrup, the cooled sugar syrup and the grapefruit juice and process into a smooth purée. Stir in the rum, if using.

Strain through a fine sieve, then transfer to an ice cream machine and freeze according to the manufacturer's instructions. Freeze if not using immediately.

For the float, cut away the peel and white pith from all the citrus fruits, then segment the orange and grapefruit. Set aside.

In a small pan, gently heat the ginger and its syrup along with the lemongrass and mint for about 1 minute. Strain and set aside to cool.

To serve, place 1 or 2 scoops of the prepared lychee sorbet in a suitable martini or tumbler-style glass. Top with the fruit and drizzle the cooled ginger syrup over the top. Finally, pour in the soda and serve immediately while it is still bubbling.

4 PORTIONS: 227 CALS, 1.5G PROTEIN, 0.2G FAT, 0G SATURATED FAT, 58.3G CARBOHYDRATE, 57.6G SUGAR, 2G FIBER, 23MG SODIUM

lemon verbena and berry gratin

Lemon verbena is a wonderful plant: by no means attractive or showy, it imports a fantastic lemony flavor to all kinds of dishes from poultry to desserts, salad dressings, sorbets and ice creams.

2 cups raspberries
1 cup blackberries
1 cup blueberries
4 lemon verbena leaves, shredded
1 tablespoon kirsch liqueur (optional)
2 large eggs, separated
4 tablespoons superfine sugar
juice and zest of 2 lemons
1 teaspoon cornstarch
a little confectioners' sugar, to glaze

Serves 4

Preheat the oven to 350°F.

Mix the berries in a bowl, add the shredded verbena leaves and the kirsch, if using, and cover with plastic wrap. Leave to steep for 20–30 minutes.

Meanwhile, beat the egg yolks and 2 ounces of the sugar in a bowl until light and creamy. Stir in the lemon juice and zest and add the cornstarch. Transfer to a heavy-bottomed saucepan and heat, stirring, until it almost reaches a boil and thickens (do not boil). Leave to cool, stirring occasionally so no film forms on the surface.

Whisk the egg whites with the remaining sugar until very stiff, then gently fold into the lemon sauce.

Divide the berries between 4 shallow ovenproof dishes and pour the lemon sauce over the top. Bake for 18–20 minutes or until puffed up and golden. Dust liberally with confectioner's sugar and serve.

4 PORTIONS: 141 CALS, 5G PROTEIN, 4G FAT, 0.9G SATURATED FAT, 24G CARBOHYDRATE, 22.7G SUGAR, 2.5G FIBER, 47MG SODIUM

hot cherries with red wine, licorice and yogurt sorbet

I look forward to the arrival of the first summer cherries with great excitement and all kinds of dishes are conjured up in my mind. Here is one of my favorites. People with very high blood pressure, though, should avoid eating too much licorice as it can cause a rise in blood pressure. If in doubt, check with your doctor.

zest of ½ lemon
2 tablespoons honey
⅓ cup red wine
1 tablespoon reduced-sugar redcurrant jelly
½ tablespoon licorice essence (or 2 licorice sticks, peeled and chopped)
1½ cups ripe cherries, pitted
1 tablespoon chopped pistachio nuts, to serve (optional)

For the sorbet
1¾ cups low-fat yogurt
⅓ cup 1% milk
¼ cup superfine sugar

Serves 4

For the sorbet, mix the yogurt, milk and sugar in a bowl, then transfer to an ice-cream maker and freeze following the manufacturer's instructions.

Place the zest, honey, red wine, redcurrant jelly and licorice essence in a small pan and bring to a boil. Simmer for 2–3 minutes, then add the cherries. Simmer gently, uncovered, for 5 minutes until the cherries are tender and the cooking liquid has become syrupy.

Divide the cherries between 4 individual serving bowls and top with the yogurt sorbet. Sprinkle with the chopped pistachios if using. Serve immediately.

4 PORTIONS: 197 CALS, 6.8G PROTEIN, 1.5G FAT, 0.9G SATURATED FAT, 39.5G CARBOHYDRATE, 39.2G SUGAR, 0.8G FIBER, 91MG SODIUM

eton mess
(an italian version)

Here's a play on the classic British dessert Eton Mess, usually comprising crushed fluffy meringue, soft raspberries and cream. In my version I add some dramatic flair while retaining the original concept. I think you will enjoy it.

4 large ripe peaches
4 small ready-made meringue nests
1 cup low-fat fromage frais
4 amaretti biscuits, crushed
1 tablespoon Amaretto liqueur (optional)
cocoa powder, for dusting

Serves 4

Place the peaches in a bowl, cover with boiling water, let sit for 1 minute, then remove with a slotted spoon. Peel and cut the peaches in half, remove the pits, then cut into large cubes and set aside.

In a bowl, crush the meringue into large pieces, add the fromage frais, crushed amaretti biscuits and liqueur, if using. Add two-thirds of the peaches and gently fold together.

Spoon the mixture into 4 individual tumbler-style glasses. Top with the remaining peaches and dust lightly with a little cocoa powder to serve.

4 PORTIONS: 176 CALS, 8G PROTEIN, 1G FAT, 0.4G SATURATED FAT, 35G CARBOHYDRATE, 31G SUGAR, 2.5G FIBER, 75MG SODIUM

lemon polenta cake with figs

Polenta (or cornmeal) is often used in desserts in Italy and works extremely well. Some brands, however, contain salt, so check the label. The tanginess of the lemon syrup with figs brings the whole thing together wonderfully well. Using poached pears or kumquats would also be very good.

6 eggs, separated
⅔ cup superfine sugar
⅔ cup low-fat plain yogurt
zest and juice of 2 lemons
3½ ounces polenta (ground cornmeal)
1 teaspoon low-sodium baking powder
⅔ cup ground almonds
4 firm ripe figs, cut into quarters
2 tablespoons slivered almonds, lightly toasted

For the lemon syrup
4 lemons
2 tablespoons maple syrup
⅓ cup water

Serves 8

Preheat the oven to 350°F. Lightly grease a 7-inch cake pan, square or round and line the bottom with parchment paper.

To make the cake, beat the egg yolks in a bowl, add the sugar and whisk until light, thick and creamy. Add the yogurt, lemon juice and zest. Using a metal spoon, fold in the polenta, baking powder and ground almonds.

In a separate bowl, whisk the egg whites until stiff, then carefully fold into the yogurt mix (do not overmix).

Spoon the mix into the prepared cake tin, smooth and level off the top. Bake for 30–40 minutes until golden and the cake is cooked through when tested with the point of a small knife. Allow to cool slightly before turning out onto a cooling rack.

For the syrup, zest 2 of the lemons and squeeze the juice from all 4. Combine this with the syrup and water in a small pan and simmer for 2–3 minutes.

Cut the cake into squares or slices, top each with 2 fig quarters, drizzle with the warm lemon syrup and scatter over the toasted almonds on top. Serve.

4 PORTIONS: 348 CALS, 12.9G PROTEIN, 17.6G FAT, 2.5G SATURATED FAT, 36.7G CARBOHYDRATE, 28.1G SUGAR, 2.3G FIBER, 117MG SODIUM

orange marmalade pudding

If you're a pudding lover like me you won't be disappointed with this recipe. The yogurt keeps it extremely light while the marmalade, which cooks in the bottom of the dish, adds a touch of bitterness, but a wonderful overall balance.

4 tablespoons margarine spread
5 tablesoons low-fat plain yogurt
6 tablespoons superfine sugar
1 teaspoon finely grated
  orange zest
2 eggs
6 tablespoons all-purpose flour
2 tablespoons cornstarch

1 teaspoon low-sodium
  baking powder
⅓ cup maple syrup
4 tablespoons reduced-sugar
  orange marmalade
confectioners' sugar, to dust
low-fat plain yogurt or low-fat
  vanilla ice cream, to serve

Serves 6

Preheat the oven to 350°F.

Lightly grease the inside of 6 individual soufflé or ramekin dishes. In a bowl, whisk together the spread, yogurt, sugar and zest until light and fluffy. Whisk in the eggs one at a time. In a separate bowl, sift the flour, cornstarch and baking powder together, then fold into the wet mixture.

Mix the maple syrup and marmalade together in a bowl, then divide the mix into the bottom of the prepared dishes. Carefully spoon the pudding mix over the marmalade and fill them up to the top of each dish.

Cover the dishes with plastic wrap and place in a deep-sided baking pan. Pour enough boiling water into the pan to reach halfway up the sides of the ramekins.

Cover the pan, return the water to a boil, then reduce the heat to a simmer. Cook for 25–30 minutes or until a small knife inserted in the center of a pudding comes out clean. Carefully remove the puddings and allow to cool slightly. Dust liberally with confectioner's sugar and serve warm with low-fat yogurt or vanilla ice cream.

4 PORTIONS: 270 CALS, 5G PROTEIN, 8G FAT, 1.9G SATURATED FAT, 47G CARBOHYDRATE, 29.6G SUGAR, 0.5G FIBER, 153MG SODIUM

summer fruit piperade

A piperade is a typical savory dish from the Basque region of Europe made of peppers, onions and tomatoes cooked in olive oil and mixed with eggs—the colors represent those in the Basque flag. In this sweet version I use fruit instead of vegetables. It makes an unusual dessert and is one that can be produced quickly.

1 teaspoon unsalted butter
2 tablespoons superfine sugar
½ cup blackberries
½ cup raspberries
⅓ cup blueberries
6 eggs
1 small vanilla pod, split, seeds removed
  (or ½ teaspoon vanilla extract)
1 tablespoon kirsch (cherry liqueur)
2 tablespoons lightly toasted slivered almonds
confectioners' sugar, to dust
low-fat fromage frais, to serve

Serves 4

Preheat the broiler on high. Heat the butter in a medium-sized, ovenproof, non-stick pan. Add 1 teaspoon of the sugar and the fruit and toss together in the pan for 1 minute.

In a bowl whisk the eggs with the remaining sugar, vanilla seeds or extract and kirsch, if using. Pour the eggs over the fruit and stir gently with a fork as if making an omelette, until eggs are lightly set.

Sprinkle with the flaked almonds, dust liberally all over with confectioner's sugar, then place under the broiler until the sugar is lightly caramelized and golden. Carefully slip the omelette out of the pan onto a large serving plate and dust with more sugar. Serve with low-fat fromage frais.

4 PORTIONS: 288 CALS, 13G PROTEIN, 14G FAT, 3.6G SATURATED FAT, 26G CARBOHYDRATE, 26.2G SUGAR, 2.7G FIBER, 131MG SODIUM

strawberry and watermelon gelatin with sweet pesto

I love the freshness of this dessert, which should ideally only be made in the height of summer when local strawberries are sweet, juicy and utterly delicious.

2¼ cups ripe but firm strawberries,
  hulled and halved
1¼ cups watermelon, skin removed
  and cut into cubes
2 tablespoons superfine sugar
4 gelatin leaves (or 1 tablespoon granulated gelatin)
⅓ cup rosé wine (or champagne!)

Serves 4

Place half of the strawberries and watermelon in a bowl and cover with the sugar and ⅔ cup of water. Place the bowl above a pan of simmering water and leave to cook for 1½ hours, by which time the strawberries will have released their natural juices.

Remove the bowl and strain the juices through a fine sieve (or coffee filter) so you are left with a clear, sweet juice. Soak the gelatin leaves in a bowl of cold water for 4–5 minutes to soften. Measure ⅔ cup of the juice and heat gently in a pan. Squeeze the gelatin leaves out in your hand, add to the juice and stir well until melted. Add the wine and transfer to a bowl to cool slightly.

Meanwhile, place the remaining strawberries and watermelon in shallow soup-style serving bowls or glasses. Top with the juice and place in fridge for about 30 minutes to set.

For the sweet pesto, place all the ingredients in a blender and process into a coarse texture. Top the gelatins with a dollop of fromage frais, drizzle the sweet pesto on top and serve.

4 PORTIONS: 204 CALS, 8G PROTEIN, 3G FAT, 0.2G SATURATED FAT, 35G CARBOHYDRATE, 33.3G SUGAR, 1.8G FIBER, 32MG SODIUM

pear, rhubarb and cranberry crumble

A melange of sweet and sour-tasting fruits that combine together wonderfully, topped with a crisp oatmeal crust. Crumbles are so diverse and, let's face it, are loved by all. Other variations could be the addition of a little chopped candied ginger to the fruits or a blend of mixed nuts added to the crust. Why not create your own?!

3 ripe firm pears, peeled and cored
2¼ cups rhubarb, trimmed and cut into 1-inch lengths
2 tablespoons brown sugar
zest of 1 orange
1¼ cups fresh (or frozen) cranberries
½ cup cranberry juice

For the crumble
6 tablespoons whole grain flour
4 tablespoons rolled oats
4 tablespoons brown sugar
4 tablespoons ground hazelnuts
4 tablespoons margarine spread, warmed

Serves 4

Preheat oven to 400°F.

Chop the pears into large pieces and place in a shallow ovenproof dish. Add the rhubarb, sugar, orange zest and cranberries and pour in the cranberry juice. Combine well and bake for 10 minutes.

Meanwhile, make the crumble. In a bowl combine the flour, oats, sugar and hazelnuts. Combine the mixture until it resembles breadcrumbs in texture. Remove the fruit from the oven and sprinkle the crumble mix on top, pressing down lightly into the fruit.

Bake for 25 minutes until bubbling and golden. Serve with low-fat yogurt or low-fat fromage frais.

4 PORTIONS: 447 CALS, 8G PROTEIN, 18G FAT, 2.6G SATURATED FAT, 67G CARBOHYDRATE, 46.7G SUGAR, 9.8G FIBER, 122MG SODIUM

pecan bread pudding with banana sorbet

When I was a child growing up in England, bread pudding was a regular treat that my mother made. Its a great way to use up any stale bread left over, though there wasn't much with three children! I thought it was time to give this dish it's due! I have infused a little decadence with the addition of chopped pecans, but they could be left out in honor of tradition. This sorbet is made easily in the freezer and does not require an ice cream machine.

1 cup whole grain bread, ideally stale
6 tablespoons mixed dried fruits (currants, raisins, etc)
3 tablespoons light brown sugar
3 tablespoons suet or vegetable shortening
1 teaspoon pumpkin pie spice
1 large egg, beaten
a little 1% milk
1¼ cups pecans, lightly crushed (optional)
confectioners' sugar, to taste

For the sorbet
¾ cup superfine sugar
⅔ cup spring water
¾ cup ripe banana, chopped
juice of ½ lemon

Serves 6

First make the sorbet. Place the sugar and water in a large pan and bring to a boil slowly to dissolve the sugar completely. Remove from the heat and allow to cool.

When cool, add the banana and lemon juice, transfer to a suitable freezer container and freeze for about 3 hours, until set around the edges.

Transfer the sorbet to a small blender and process until smooth. Return to the freezer until gently set; this will take 2–2½ hours. It is then ready for use.

Preheat the oven to 325°F.

Cut or tear the bread into small chunks and place in a bowl. Add a little water just to cover and leave to soak for 45 minutes. Squeeze out the bread as dry as possible with your hands. Place in a bowl, add the fruit, suet (or shortening), sugar and spice and mix well. Add the egg and enough milk until the batter drops off a spoon.

Sprinkle the pecans over the bottom of a lightly greased baking pan and then carefully pour in the bread mixture. Bake for 1–1¼ hours until browned—it should be slightly firm to the touch. Leave to cool a while before removing from the pan.

Cut into small squares, dust with confectioners' sugar and serve with the banana sorbet.

6 PORTIONS: 415 CALS, 5.8G PROTEIN, 9.7G FAT, 0.6G SATURATED FAT, 81.3G CARBOHYDRATE, 64.7G SUGAR, 2.7G FIBER, 119MG SODIUM

pineapple and raisin clafoutis with curry ice cream

Traditional French clafoutis is made with sweet cherries, which is wonderful—the French often like it for a sweet breakfast treat. Any fruit can be used; here I use pineapple, which is available ready-prepared in many good supermarkets. The curry ice cream works wonderfully with the hot custard: don't be put off by the thought of it on first glance, it's a real dinner party centerpiece.

3 large eggs
1 tablespoon superfine sugar
1 tablespoon cornstarch
2 tablespoons custard powder
1⅓ cups 1% milk
1 tablespoon ground almonds
⅓ cup raisins, soaked in warm water for
    30 minutes, drained and dried
1 cup ready-prepared fresh pineapple,
    cut into large chunks

for the ice cream
1 cup 1% milk
1 teaspoon mild curry powder
4 egg yolks
6 tablespoons superfine sugar

Serves 4

First make the ice cream. Bring the milk and curry powder to a boil in a saucepan, then remove from the heat and leave to cool slightly. In a large bowl, whisk the egg yolks and sugar until light, fluffy and doubled in volume. Pour in the cooled milk, whisking constantly. Leave to cool completely, stirring occasionally.

When cooled, pour into an ice-cream machine and freeze following the manufacturer's instructions. Freeze until needed.

For the clafoutis, preheat the oven to 350°F. Place all the ingredients except the raisins and the pineapple in a mixing bowl and, using an electric beater or whisk, beat to a smooth batter. Stir in the raisins and leave the batter to sit for 15 minutes.

Divide the pineapple cubes equally between 4 individual baking dishes, then pour the sweet batter over the top each.

Bake for 25–30 minutes until golden. Allow to cool slightly. Top with a ball of curry ice cream and serve. If you're still not sure, vanilla ice cream works well, too!

4 PORTIONS: 497 CALS, 17G PROTEIN, 16G FAT, 5.2G SATURATED FAT, 75G CARBOHYDRATE, 68.1G SUGAR, 1.6G FIBER, 189MG SODIUM

sweet fennel risotto

Fennel? In a dessert, you say?! Don't knock it until you've tried it! Blanching the rice in the first stages of the recipe gives a less starchy grain and, to me, improves the final result. This is delicious served cold, but I prefer it warm topped with fruit such as pears and apples. It makes a lovely warm and different dessert to serve on a cold winter night.

¾ cup risotto rice (e.g. arborio)
1 tablespoon unsalted butter (optional) or 1 tablespoon canola oil
4 tablespoons superfine sugar
1 head fennel, trimmed and cut into small dice
⅓ cup fresh or store-bought pear juice
1 vanilla pod, halved and seeds removed
    (or 1 teaspoon vanilla extract)
2 cups 1% milk, hot
4 tablespoons raisins, soaked in water for 30 minutes until plump,
    drained and dried
½–1 pear, thinly sliced

Serves 4

Place the rice in a saucepan, pour in enough boiling water to cover. Simmer for 5 minutes, uncovered, then drain in a colander. Gently rinse the rice under slow running water and set aside.

In a heavy-bottomed pan, heat the butter and half of the sugar. When melted, add the fennel and cook over a low heat for 10–12 minutes until the fennel is tender and lightly caramelized.

Add the pear juice, remaining sugar, vanilla seeds and pods and bring to a boil. Add the hot milk and the blanched rice, reduce the heat and simmer for another 20 minutes, stirring often, until the rice is cooked, creamy and still retaining a little bite (al dente).

Stir in the soaked raisins, then divide between 4 serving bowls. Fan the thinly sliced raw pear on top of the risotto and serve.

4 PORTIONS: 326 CALS, 9G PROTEIN, 6G FAT, 1.8G SATURATED FAT, 64G CARBOHYDRATE, 34.5G SUGAR, 2.2G FIBER, 81MG SODIUM

syrian winter fruits with saffron yogurt

To me dried fruits are very underrated, which is a shame, particularly as most (though not prunes) are high in potassium, which has the opposite effect in the body to sodium and helps reduce blood pressure! Here they are served warm with an aromatically flavored saffron yogurt spiked with green cardamom. Dried limes are available from Middle Eastern stores, wonderful in many dishes of Arabic origin.

1 cup orange juice
juice and zest of 1 lemon
1 cinnamon stick
½ teaspoon ginger, chopped
2 tablespoons honey
1 dried lime, halved (optional)
1¾ cups ready-to-eat dried fruit
    (e.g. prunes, apricots, figs)

For the saffron yogurt
½ cup low-fat plain yogurt
1 teaspoon cornstarch
½ teaspoon ground cardamom
good pinch of saffron (fresh
    or powder)

Serves 4

First heat the yogurt, saffron and cornstarch together in a pan until it reaches a boil, stirring constantly. Cook for 1 minute, add the cardamom and transfer to a bowl. Cool, then refrigerate for up to 2 hours.

For the fruit place the orange juice, lemon juice and zest, cinnamon, ginger, honey and dried lime in a pan. Bring to a boil then lower the heat and simmer for 5 minutes. Add the dried fruit, return to a boil, remove from the heat and leave to cool. Remove the fruit from the liquid then strain the poaching liquid. Return the poaching liquid to the pan and reduce it over medium heat until it reaches a syrup consistency.

To serve, warm the fruit gently in the syrup and divide between 4 serving dishes. Place a dollop of saffron yogurt to one side and serve.

4 PORTIONS: 242 CALS, 5G PROTEIN, 1G FAT, 0.2G SATURATED FAT, 56G CARBOHYDRATE, 54.4G SUGAR, 6.4G FIBER, 56MG SODIUM

vanilla brûlée with prunes in cognac

Everyone loves crème brûlée, traditionally made rich with heavy cream. My healthier version uses only milk, but with the vanilla and the Cognac prunes is still packed with flavor. The prunes are best made well in advance.

For the brûlée
1 large vanilla pod, split
  (or 1 teaspoon vanilla extract)
2 cups 1% milk, plus 2 tablespoons
2 tablespoons custard powder
6 egg yolks
⅓ cup superfine sugar
1 tablespoon extra sugar, to glaze the brûlée

For the prunes
2 tablespoons maple syrup
12 large prunes, pitted and ready to eat
1 tablespoon Cognac

Serves 4

For the prunes, bring the maple syrup and ⅓ cup water to a boil and simmer for 5 minutes. Add the prunes and simmer for another 5 minutes, then remove from the heat. Add the Cognac and allow to cool. Keep in a sealed container in the fridge. Note: the longer the prunes are left in the syrup, the better the flavor. They will keep well for up to a week.

For the brûlée, using a small knife, scrape the seeds from the vanilla pod, add to the 2 cups of milk in a small pan, then bring gently to a boil. Mix the custard powder with the extra 2 tablespoons milk, then whisk into the warm milk. Remove from the heat.

In a bowl, whisk the egg yolks and sugar together, beating until light and fluffy. Slowly whisk the thickened custard into the egg and whisk until smooth and creamy.

Return the custard to the stove over very low heat and cook until the custard is at 172°F (do not let it boil or curdle). Remove from the heat then strain through a fine sieve. Cool slightly. Pour into 4 gratin-style dishes and place in the fridge for 2–3 hours to set.

To serve, remove from the fridge, sprinkle liberally with sugar and, using a kitchen blowtorch or under a preheated hot broiler, glaze until golden.

Leave to cool about 2 minutes until the sugar crust has hardened. Serve with the Cognac prunes on the side.

4 PORTIONS: 373 CALS, 12G PROTEIN, 13G FAT, 4.4G SATURATED FAT, 54G CARBOHYDRATE, 48.6G SUGAR, 2.1G FIBER, 107MG SODIUM

stuffed baked apples with vanilla-cardamom yogurt

When I was young, baked apples were a regular option for dessert. Nowadays with all the various fruits we have available to buy and at our disposal, they have fallen from favor.

4 russet or Golden Delicious
  apples, stems removed
⅓ cup dates, coarsely chopped
2 tablespoons slivered almonds
2 tablespoons shelled
  pistachio nuts
1 tablespoon brown sugar
juice of ½ lemon

For the vanilla-cardamom yogurt
⅓ cup low-fat plain yogurt
1 vanilla pod, halved, seeds
  removed (or 1 teaspoon
  vanilla extract)
½ teaspoon ground cardamom
1 tablespoon maple syrup
pinch of ground cinnamon

Serves 4

Preheat the oven to 350°F.

Core the apples with an apple corer, ensuring there are no seeds or core remaining. You should have a clean, clear tunnel through the middle from top to bottom.

In a bowl, mix together the remaining ingredients, then fill the center of each apple with the mixture, pressing down to ensure the center of each apple is tightly filled. Place on a lightly greased baking pan.

Spoon 1 tablespoon of hot water over each apple, then bake for 30–35 minutes until the apples are tender.

Meanwhile, combine all the ingredients for the vanilla-cardamom yogurt in a bowl. Refrigerate until needed.

Serve the stuffed apples while warm with the yogurt sauce spooned over them.

4 PORTIONS: 447 CALS, 8G PROTEIN, 18G FAT, 2.6G SATURATED FAT, 67G CARBOHYDRATE, 46.7G SUGAR, 9.8G FIBER, 122MG SODIUM

asian-style oranges with almond praline

When the blood orange season begins I often use them to prepare this dish, as their color is so dramatic.

4 juicy medium-large oranges
3 tablespoons maple syrup
1 stalk lemongrass, outer husk
  removed, inner core finely
  chopped
½ teaspoon chopped red chile
2 star anise pods
4 passion fruits, halved, juice
  and seeds separated

1 small piece preserved ginger,
  finely chopped, plus
  1 teaspoon syrup from the jar

For the praline
⅔ cup superfine sugar
¼ cup slivered almonds
seeds from passion fruits
  (see above)

Serves 4

For the praline, place the sugar and 3 tablespoons of water in a small heavy-bottomed pan and cook over low heat until the sugar has dissolved. Without stirring, bring to a boil until the sugar caramelizes and becomes golden in color. Remove from the heat, stir in the almonds and passion fruit seeds. Pour into a small baking pan lined with parchment paper and leave to harden. Break into large pieces and set aside.

For the oranges, reserve the zest of one orange then remove the peels from all the oranges and cut into thick slices.

Place the maple syrup, lemongrass, chile, star anise, orange zest and ½ cup water in a pot and simmer for 5 minutes. Remove from heat, add the passion fruit juice and chopped ginger and syrup.

Arrange the orange slices on a deep plate, slightly overlapping one another, pour the syrup over the top and chill until ready to serve. Top the oranges with the almond praline and serve chilled.

4 PORTIONS: 303 CALS, 4G PROTEIN, 9G FAT, 0.6G SATURATED FAT, 56G CARBOHYDRATE, 54.4G SUGAR, 2.3G FIBER, 11MG SODIUM

wild berry cranachan

Made with low-fat yogurt instead of the usual cream, this traditional Scottish dessert is often served during New Year's Eve, weddings or other special occasions. Use a good brand of vanilla extract here, its worth the expense!

⅓ cup rolled oats
1 cup low-fat plain yogurt
1 tablespoon reduced-sugar raspberry jam
1 teaspoon vanilla extract
1 tablespoon honey
1 tablespoon whisky

1¼ cups mixed wild berries of your choice (e.g. blueberries, blackberries, raspberries)

Serves 4

Place the oats in a hot, dry non-stick pan, and toast for about 1 minute until lightly golden (alternatively, spread the oats out on a baking sheet and place under a hot broiler).

In a bowl, mix the yogurt, jam, vanilla, honey and whisky. Crush 1 cup of the fruit lightly in a bowl, then gently fold in the yogurt mix. Finally fold in the toasted oats, leaving a few to garnish the top, using a metal spoon to give a rippled effect.

Transfer to tall glasses, top with the remaining berries, sprinkle with the remaining toasted oats and serve.

4 PORTIONS: 180 CALS, 8G PROTEIN, 3G FAT, 0.7G SATURATED FAT, 31G CARBOHYDRATE, 14G SUGAR, 4.5G FIBER, 48MG SODIUM

stock bases

You will notice that I use a lot of freshly made stocks in my recipes. The reason for this is two fold:

Firstly, commercial bouillon cubes are rather salty in flavor, thereby defeating the object of reducing your salt intake and secondly, homemade stocks not only taste better but give a much better flavor to the dish you are cooking.

There are some fairly acceptable prepared, packaged stocks available from leading supermarkets and gourmet markets but make sure you look out for the reduced-sodium varieties. If you must use bouillon cubes, I recommend only half a cube per 2 cups of liquid.

Homemade stocks take very little time and effort to make and can be prepared in advance, kept covered in the fridge for up to 4 days or in the freezer for up to 3 months, in small quantities.

chicken stock

4½ pounds chicken bones
2 medium onions, chopped
2 celery stalks, chopped
1 bay leaf
2 medium carrots, chopped
2 teaspoons black peppercorns
1⅓ gallons water

Combine all the ingredients in a large pot, bring to a boil and skim off any impurities which rise to the surface. Simmer for 2 hours, then strain (makes 10½ cups).

reduced chicken stock

Like the chicken stock but first we roast all the dry ingredients in the oven for 30 minutes with 1 tablespoon tomato paste until golden. Drain off any excess fat, then place in a pot and simmer for 2 hours, then strain.

Place in a pot, bring to a boil and simmer until the liquid has reduced by half (makes 6⅓ cups). This will give a darker, more complex flavor that is often used in sauce bases.

fish stock

3⅓ pounds fish bones
1 medium onion, chopped
2 celery stalks, chopped
1 bay leaf
½ teaspoon black peppercorns
1½ gallons water

Combine all the ingredients in a large pot and bring to a boil. Simmer uncovered for 20 minutes, skimming off the impurities that rise to the surface, then strain (makes 10½ cups).

vegetable stock

1 large carrot, chopped
1 large parsnip, chopped
2 medium onions, chopped
2 carrots, chopped
2 celery stalks, chopped
1 bay leaf
1 teaspoon black peppercorns
1½ gallons water

Combine all the ingredients in a large pot, bring to a boil, simmer uncovered for 1 hour, then strain (makes 10½ cups).

index

acknowledgments

Working on this book has not only been an enjoyable culinary challenge but also extremely educational for me and having the support of Gemma Heiser has benefited the book no end. Thank you Gemma for all your knowledge and support.

As always, my heartfelt thanks go to home economist and friend Linda Tubby and photographer Will Heap. Thank you both for your boundless enthusiasm, passion and dedication to this project.

Thanks also to Wendy Doyle for analysing the recipes from a nutritional standpoint, Roisin Nield for her beautiful prop styling, Geoff Hayes, for his stunning book design, and Gemma John, for taking care of the production side of things.

Many thanks to Lara Mand, my PA, for her help in formulating the backbone of the recipes in the early stages.

And finally, a huge thank you to Judith Hannam, editor, and Vicki Murrell, editorial assistant, for their invaluable support and friendship. Working with you both has been effortless and a real pleasure. You helped see the project through every stage and I am very grateful to you both for making it all happen.